A Field Guide to Earthlings:
An autistic/Asperger view of neurotypical behavior

Covers nuances of friendship, dating, small talk, interpersonal conflicts, image, learning styles, social communication, common sense, white lies, and much more!

by Ian Ford

Illustrated by Stephanie Hamilton

Credits: Illustrations by Stephanie Hamilton. Cover art by
Brianna Petersen. Cover design by Adam Ford. Cover
photo by Space Telescope Science Institute
(www.hubblesite.org). Photo of marching band by Terry
Shuck, available under the Creative Commons Attribution
2.0 Generic license
(http://creativecommons.org/licenses/by/2.0/deed.en).

Publisher:
        Ian Ford Software Corporation, Albuquerque, NM
        www.ianford.com
Book's web site: www.afieldguidetoearthlings.com

ISBN: 9780615426198
Library of Congress Control Number: 2010918011

First printing: December 2010

Contents

Introduction

Hello! This book reveals psychological patterns of **neurotypical** (NT) humans, from an autistic perspective. I wrote it to help you understand them. You might read it if you are autistic (or Asperger's) and have to work harder to understand why people do what they do, or you might read it if you are neurotypical and want to understand an autistic person in your life, or you might read it because you are interested in new ways of looking at personalities and behavior.

A large majority of people are neurotypical. The word "neurotypical" (or NT) is not derogatory or complimentary - it is neutral. The label is not normally used by people to describe themselves, but is often used from an autistic perspective to name those people who are not labeled as autistic, ADD, ADHD, or any other specific neurological condition.

I've spent the last 42 years living among and studying these curious creatures. It has been a difficult life, and actually not one that I would have chosen. I will restrict my autobiography to a single paragraph, so that I don't lose my readers too early on. I first arrived on Earth through the labors of my mother, who gave me milk, and, later, piano lessons. I went to preschool with Andrea, and I remember there was a vague mass of other children whose names didn't interest me. I learned to play sonatinas, make tri-fold display boards for science fair projects, and several other things that resulted in childhood honors. I made tree forts with my friend Sarah. My inner life was only open to a select few including her and my cousin Emily. My parents went along with my androgynous ways and my demands for order, and they never started talking about making them proud until it was far too late. Other people, of whom I had limited use, were strangely offended at my unexamined assumption that I was great, and I felt they kept getting in the way of its fruition. I was lost and depressed during the first seven years of my eternal adolescence, punctuated by brief and deep friendships like Melissa with whom meaning flowed out into the world around us, and by my trip to Africa where I was nearly comatose on the outside but was secretly ecstatic. Believing mutual love was unlikely, I married my first "girlfriend" after a reasoned cost-benefit analysis, and had one daughter. I had retained my girlhood innocence and a save-the-world idealism that fueled a series of philanthropic projects and efforts to belong, all of which upset someone's apple cart and ended with me being ejected back into anonymity. I was weak, defenseless, and apparently dangerous. All of this was before I found out they were neurotypical and I was not. I'm now married again and live fairly peacefully with a wife, daughter and stepdaughter.

The 62 patterns in this book will explain what I've learned from my observations, colored as they are by my involvement in the subjects of my study. It will show how and why NTs live in complex competitive social structures, why they have elaborate mating rituals, how they display feelings for intentional effect, and it will reveal many more fascinating abilities of the species.

It is organized from the ground up: the physical and perceptive functions first, then the inner workings of the mind, then building to the NT's relationships and roles in the wider world. It also contains the script of a play whose ten scenes provide some examples of the patterns.

My hope is that you will be able to get the patterns fixed in your mind through my explanations, plus from the dialog in the play, then as you go about your life, you will recognize the patterns in the people around you. In the past I have seen NTs negatively as just a weak-minded herd of clones who waste all their time pointlessly talking about nothing, but I've begun to see them more positively as a result of understanding their "wiring." This book might help you see what they are doing in a more forgiving and deeper way, and help you understand why the time they spend doing those NT things is not actually a waste. After reading the book, you might be somewhere (a place you've been before) and see people interacting (like they have before) but you may see it in a new light. You might recognize a pattern from the book, and you might stop seeing the NTs as being so pointless or mystifying.

If you get lost in the abstractions of the 62 patterns, you might skip ahead to the last section, "What's an autie to do," which has personal advice on topics such as loneliness and authenticity. This kind of autistic-oriented advice is rare to nonexistent in self help books, and I hope that this unique section of the book will be helpful to you.

Language and culture

Before we get into the explanation of NTs, we must first define some terms related to language and culture. NTs are all about culture; culture is an extension of language, and so we begin with clarity about language.

Linguists refer to **"signs"** as the most general concept that includes words, gestures, icons, and other cultural symbols. In this book we will not get into linguistics in much detail, and will just use the term **"symbol"** for all of those concepts. Thus, a word is a symbol, a cheer or other non-word sound is a symbol, and a hand gesture or intentional pose is a symbol. We will also include cultural patterns as symbols, such as styles of dress, events, architectural styles, sports, political views, and anything else that can be named and has a culturally specific meaning. By culturally specific, we mean something that means or could mean something else in a different culture. For example, in one culture, turning a dinner cup upside down could mean you don't want any more drink, but in another culture it could mean you are insulting the cook. So, the act of turning a cup upside down is a culturally significant symbol.

A symbol has two sides: the signifier and the signified. The **signifier** is the word or other shortcut that refers to the **signified**, which is the meaning or the thing represented by the word. "Rabbit" is a word (signifier) pointing to all actual rabbits (signifieds).

rabbit
signifier

signified

A symbol consists of a signifier and a signified.

There is a difference between symbols in the cultural sense and the names of natural things. A pine cone, for example, existed before people named it and is thus not a symbol in that sense. But people also have associations and expectations about pine cones. Displaying a pine cone on the counter in a post office could mean something, so in that sense it is also a cultural symbol. There are very **concrete symbols** such as the names of plants, and more **abstract symbols** such as words describing parliamentary procedure or the display of a pine cone.

Culture can be defined as all the symbols that a group of people share, including but not limited to words.

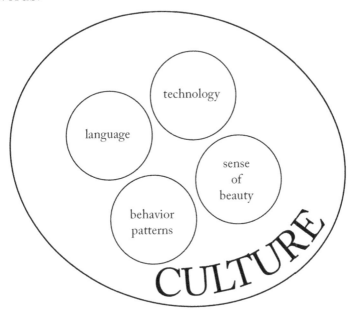

Some components of culture.

Semantics is the area of linguistics dealing with meaning. Linguists divide the study of language into phonology (units of sound), morphology (structure of words), lexicology (words), syntax (grammar), semantics (meaning), and pragmatics (context), among others.

The **symbolic web** is the mental representation of all known symbols and their connections. It is like a memorized dictionary, except instead of being arranged alphabetically, it is arranged organically as a web of connections between symbols.

Associations are mental connections that form the symbolic web. Associations can be based on words that have sounds in common (milk and silk, panda and pan), symbols that you learned at the same time in your life, symbols relating to a person or place that is important to you, symbols having related meanings (ink and pen), or symbols having related contexts (steak and eggs).

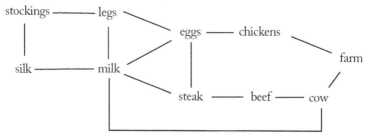

One tiny part of a symbolic web.

Some symbols have no clear signified; they are semantically starved, which is to say they don't mean much in any literal sense, but they are still symbols in the symbolic web. These are referred to later in the book as **free-floating cultural symbols**, such as "Victorian" and "gourmet." Their main purpose is to be associated with other symbols, rather than to refer to any real thing in the world.

Free-floating symbol.

In communication, only the symbols can cross the boundary between one person's mind and another's. The signified (what they mean) cannot cross the boundary. Each person has to build their associations independently and tie together the symbols with what they perceive to exist. Through years of communication, people living in the same environment will come know nearly the same set of symbols, and will have similar associations among them. That is, they will share the same culture. Having the same culture means having similar symbolic webs. But the meaning (signified) of abstract and free-floating symbols may be understood quite differently by different people.

People sharing the same symbolic web share the same culture.

Patterns of Perception

NT perception is restricted by their use of language and cultural symbols. (That last sentence is quite possibly the most important one in the book, although it may not be clear yet.) After the first scene of the play, we'll dive into the list of NT patterns, starting with patterns of perception.

Scene 1 of The Lockstep Tragedy

We introduce a theatrical play at this point in the book. You will see that the book switches back and forth between a work of fiction (the play) and a work of non-fiction (the explanation of NT patterns). They are interleaved so that one scene of the play is given, which demonstrates some of the NT patterns, then those patterns are explained. There are ten scenes. The sequence of the patterns is important, as each pattern builds on the prior ones, and the play had to be devised to follow that sequence. The play is also meant to be a play in its own right, with a story line, conflict, and resolution; however, it would probably not make a very compelling stage production because it is intentionally constrained by the need to expose the sequence of patterns.

One aspect of great literature that fascinates me is the way characters are bound to their particular fates, which are a result of their particular psychological blind spots and story lines. A psychological story line is like "I get no respect" or "I can't" or even "I've always depended on the kindness of strangers." I've tried to show these kinds of fates in this play, and the idea of "lockstep" is exactly that. The lockstep pattern is one of the patterns later in the book that explains the inability of groups of people to adapt.

If you study personality typing systems, you may notice that the nine main characters are all based on different types. This is really the central irony of an autistic's quest to understand NTs: They are all different, yet they move in herds. They have a common language and common rules, but they often misunderstand each other, splinter into subgroups, and often break their own rules.

*Here are the characters: **Antonio Whitting** is a heavy, jovial American sports fan who gets his steak done the way he wants his steak done. His wife **Donna** runs the household and dresses impeccably, even for housework. She and the two daughters are not at all thin, all with black straight hair. The older daughter is **Star**, a reserved, plain and peaceful girl who might be seen holding something special or pressing it tightly against her. Star is pregnant. The younger is **Angel**, who is generally seen with her hair over her face, watching. Star's friend **Valerie** is a cheerleader in life. Antonio's friend **Paul** is usually nearly smiling, and might be caught putting things back where they go while whistling. Paul's son **Ivan*** *(who is also Star's fiance) is a quiet one who is often seen looking inquisitive or lost, and is drawn to Star like a magnet. Paul's girlfriend is* **Carmen***, who is wiry with curly dyed hair and bold makeup, and has a puppy's boundless and undirected energy. Carmen employs* **James***, a factual and efficiently-moving post-adolescent who rarely removes his baseball cap.*

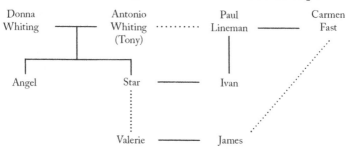

Map of the characters.
Solid lines are familial or love relationships.
Paul and Antonio are friends, Star and Valerie are friends,
and James works for Carmen.

It is summer. Donna Whiting is driving with her daughters Star and Angel, to the flower shop to finalize the flowers for Star's wedding. Traffic is stopped. Trucks are blocking the driving lanes. Windows are rolled down. Amidst horns and yelling, real estate speculator Carmen Fast is overheard arguing against a group of people in the road, who are protesting against a construction project.

ANGEL: What's the problem?

DONNA: It's just gridlock with all those trucks in the way. We can't move. The blondie in that SUV is signaling but the foreman there is apparently too busy handling that beagle to - wait, there's a cop. [*police squawk*] [*to herself, as if speaking to the police*] I see you mean for me to go around, sir, but I'd hit the dog. [*to herself*] This is no place for townhouses, and I've already given my opinion on that til I'm blue in the face.

CARMEN: [*on the sidewalk, yelling to a man*] But this is what will make it *vibrant* - The townhouses bring new opportunities. It's happening all over the country! You're literally standing in the way of progress. Maybe you can block this one truck, but *this* [*motioning to the whole construction site*] is the future. I've decided I'm getting in on the action myself - and you can't stop me. You can't stop the future!

DONNA: That one there with the red highlights [*pointing to Carmen*] was the one who talked my head off that one time about "progress." [*car moving slowly now*] I'm thinking she may be the same one Ivan's dad is with now. I don't know.

STAR: I agree with the guy. They should just leave this neighborhood alone. Watch out, mom. I'm scared for the dog.

DONNA: [*driving - to police*] Thank you sir. [*to Star*] I like that song - turn it up. We tried to stop all this - now look what a mess they are making.

The play will continue in pieces later in the book. As we go through the patterns, keep in mind that all NTs do not fit neatly into all the patterns. Everyone really is unique.

Pattern 1. Desensitization

The nearly universal pattern of desensitization means that people begin life as highly sensitive beings, then gradually learn to restrict the senses as they grow up. They cut back on detailed observation, emotional observation, and emotional response to stimuli. A desensitized NT adult can walk by blaring speakers, sirens, blinking lights and other strong stimuli without anxiety or pain.

In general, people understand that their babies are very sensitive and take in everything unfiltered, so they try not to subject babies to sharp emotional displays, loud noises, or blinking lights. But they expect that the level of sensitivity will go down with time. In addition to sensory desensitization, the emotions are also dulled; people can develop shells to protect them from nuanced emotions.

The desensitizing process happens mainly in the brain and not in the sense organs. That is, the eyes and ears still have the same ability to sense, but the brain learns to restrict the information. The conversion of actual raw perception into symbols protects the recipient from the full force of it; the world is seen through a glass darkly. It is as if people are like a pilot who only "feels" the outside rushing air indirectly by checking an airspeed dial in the cockpit. It is no longer a direct experience.

People experiencing desensitization can attempt to counter the pattern by turning up the volume in life, such as through loud music or contact sports. They also intentionally dull the senses with alcohol.

In the play, Donna and the people on the sidewalk are shown as desensitized because they can discuss things and notice things while in the presence of traffic, horns, yelling, and music. All those strong stimuli don't interfere with their perception, thinking, and communicating.

Are you sad about this? I am. The dark glass shell seems like it would be a prison, preventing direct childlike interaction with the world. But this protection is the basis for the NT's great cultural abilities, which are shown in many of the patterns later on.

Pattern 2. Symbolic filtering

The NT brain learns to categorize and direct incoming signals. NT's "catch" what comes at them; this deadens the impact. The act of deadening or filtering stimuli is called "symbolic filtering" (a term developed for this book). Symbolic filtering converts real world stimuli into an internal symbolic representation of the real world. When the external world is taken in as words, it is physically painless.

Because symbols are in the mind, the act of perception can be visualized as a collision between the internal symbolic structure coming out, and the real world coming in. The clash, or "catch," reduces the actual complexity of the stimulus by converting it into words. Perceiving is as much projecting outward as receiving inward.

The catch.

In this illustration, the viewer projects "truck" outwards when she sees the truck. In a sense, she is

21

making the big collection of metal and glass and plastic details into a single thing. In reality, it is thousands of parts; it is only a "truck" in the mind.

Another way to visualize symbolic filtering is a stencil. A beaver is pictured below, who will be play the lead role in this explanatory analogy.

Here is a photo of an actual beaver:

Here is a stencil with holes for various things that might be seen.

A stencil that includes a representation of a beaver.

The stencil is really in the mind, but can feel like it is outside the mind. The beaver image only fits through one hole, which is marked with the symbol "beaver." A myriad of rays of light from the beaver hits the stencil, but only the word "beaver" comes out the other side. This is just an analogy to help show how language works. It's a massive reduction and simplification of the data. You can think of the stencil as the mind projecting its symbolic web outwards, where it crashes into the sensory stimuli coming in, and neutralizes it.

The stencil analogy in action.

In order to use stencils that have a pattern for all possible things that may be seen, each thing has to be reduced to its "cultural sine qua non," or minimal symbolic essence. *Sine qua non* (Latin) means the aspect without which, it is nothing. For example, a beaver is only a beaver because of its unique flat tail and its upper teeth. In American culture, an animal without that tail and teeth could not be a beaver, so the aspects of the tail and the teeth are the sine qua non of the beaver. Other cultures might define it differently. Because of this phenomenon of perception, the photo could be reduced to simple cartoon drawings and still be perceived as a beaver.

In the sequence of beaver drawings below, drawings a and b encompass the sine qua non of beaverhood, because they both show the tail and upper teeth.

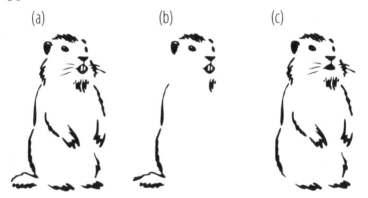

A full drawing of a beaver (a),
and two reductions of that full drawing (b and c).

Although drawing c has in fact more details of the beaver's shape than drawing b, it lacks the essential tail and teeth, and would not be as easily perceived as a beaver. I've found since I don't filter as much as NTs, that I can't identify animals very well, particularly cartoon drawings. I can see the detailed features, but can't automatically match it with a name.

All actual objects are filtered by the NT's senses into a symbol of the object. Even complex emotional states of other people are filtered into simpler symbols, protecting the recipient from the nuanced, raw feelings.

When symbolic filtering is in full force, things have to be believed to be seen. Incoming stimuli that can't be trapped by the symbolic web might simply be dropped from perception altogether. Using the stencil analogy, if there is no pre-conceived hole for the incoming stimulus to fit through, it can't be seen.

In the play, the things that Donna notices and names include an SUV, a beagle, and red highlights in someone's hair. She had to already know what these things are in order to name them quickly. When designating the foreman, she had to notice something about his uniform, possessions, or air of authority to be sure he was the foreman as opposed to some other position. She did this without stopping to think; the person's image just fit through her premade "foreman" stencil, so it was just as if she effortlessly "saw" the word "foreman."

Consider the power of symbolic filtering. All things are effortlessly compacted into their singular essence. This reduction opens up so many possibilities for the NT to manipulate and communicate these tiny, singular, data points.

Pattern 3. Multi-focus

The multi-focus pattern is active when a person is highly *efficient* at incorporating environmental data - so long as it falls within the expected cultural semantics. An NT can go into a room and instantly pick up a large number of data points, and evaluate them all. During a conversation, an NT can simultaneously *hear* and process the meaning of the words, *feel* the intent and other unspoken messages in the words, *read* the facial expressions and gestures, and *notice* other things that may be happening.

How can NTs be so powerful? There are two reasons they can do this: One is that their desensitization allows them to balance their attention without being distracted by any one overwhelming stimulus. Second, they reduce the size of the incoming data through symbolic filtering, so they only process the symbols, not the whole. Like the cockpit who is checking the airspeed dial (not actually feeling the air), they only bring in the minute essentials.

The statement above is qualified by "... that falls within the expected cultural semantics." If they go into a room where the interactions are scripted by a very foreign culture, they cannot efficiently incorporate the environment.

In the play, Donna demonstrates multi-focus because she can pick up on many things at the same time - the conversation in progress, the foreman, the dog, the trucks, the other drivers, and the police man.

Pattern 4. Sensory integration

Many NTs exhibit strong sensory integration, which is the simultaneous working together of all the senses, muscles, and associated thoughts, into one whole. The integration of all the parts balances their roles and prevents any one function from going into an overload mode.

Integration allows the person to see *all* of something complex, such as a face. Because of symbolic filtering, the parts of the face are converted into symbols (blue eyes, brown curly hair, etc.), and many of those symbols can be collected at once. NTs will often have a conscious and verbal self-knowledge of the multiple aspects. For example, seeing a familiar person at a distance, an NT might say "Is that Sandy? She has long blonde hair, glasses, and is tall, so it must be Sandy." The balanced totality of the aspects aids in recognition and recall.

Detailed ways that strong sensory integration shows itself include neat handwriting and being able to learn a dance by watching someone else do it (even if the model is facing a different direction).

Strong sensory integration is likely connected to the way NT's often learn new things in a holistic, or all-at-once kind of way, rather than as a collection of separate details. (This idea is developed later on in the forest-first learning pattern.)

By contrast, people with weaker sensory integration may allow one sense to overload, and may need a way to physically mask the strong stimulus, such as running away or self stimulation.

In the play, Donna shows strong sensory integration because she can drive and avoid a dog while at the same time having two conversations and listening to music. She does not get any of these signals crossed.

Recap

To summarize the patterns of perception, the NT's perception is both pushing out and taking in. The symbolic web is projected out from the mind onto the environment like a stencil sheet, and stimuli come in only when they fit through one of the stencils; this converts the stimulus into a symbol. Other parts of the environment that don't fit the symbolic web are not admitted. This also deadens the impact; the person is desensitized to the raw environment. Because they take in bits of information in symbolic form, NTs can process a lot of it efficiently, while also acting on it.

Patterns of Belief and Learning

This chapter looks at how the internal symbolic web is built and maintained.

This book won't distinguish much between knowledge, beliefs, propositions, concepts, and values - it's all just what goes on in the mind. The term "**belief**" will indicate all of this generally. When we talk about beliefs, we don't always mean that they are taken to be true; they might be better named "postulated beliefs" or things that exist in the mind and could be believed or disbelieved. Or, they may be preferences or ideas that a person has an alliance with.

The next scene of the play illustrates ways NTs think about things symbolically.

Scene 2 of The Lockstep Tragedy

In a flower shop. Willie, five, is holding an unusual animal with white fur. His mother is the saleswoman. Donna, Star and Angel enter.

Star: Look, Angel! [*pointing to the animal*]

Angel: What is that?

Willie: This is Cinnamon. Do you want to hold her?

Star: But I don't know what it is.

Willie: [*holding up the animal*] It's *Cinnamon*. If you hold her for a while, you'll get to know her.

Donna: Come and leave him alone now. I wish you would be more grateful for my help. You need to get more lilies for the front walk.

Star: [*to Willie*] Sorry, I need to go. [*to Donna*] Lilies? Misty didn't have any lilies. Her wedding was all red. It's all red and purple this year. [*wandering*] How about these peonies? Peonies are great. Or I know, I'll just have poinsettias.

Donna: Star child, poinsettias really! What do you want people to think? You're right about peonies though. But the wedding is Saturday and we can't change everything!

Angel: You people are lame-o's. I'm getting black roses for my wedding. Ones that draw blood.

Donna: You'll need a lot of help at your wedding, Angel. I'm sure you can do better than that.

Saleswoman: Ms. Whiting, I wanted to show you our *designer bouquet*, which is here. It's one of our *traditional essentials.* If you go with these, let's see, that's only three days away. Yes, I can have them for Saturday. As far as matching colors, I haven't seen the bridesmaids' dresses yet.

Donna: Oh! *essentials,* yes. That's nice. Star says this year is red and purple. And I suppose that *would* go with the rest.

Saleswoman: A lot of our clients are really setting forth a lively statement with the essentials of red *with white,* or in an alternative element of purple *with white.* It's totally up to you.

Star: [*to Donna*] We're traditional people, right? This one says "me" more than those. [*pointing to a bouquet*]

Donna: It says more money too. That's OK though - we *want* to pay for this. It's just... I don't know if I can put more on my credit card or not.

Star, Donna, and Saleswoman finish up business. Separated a few feet away, Angel is still talking with Willie.

Angel: I want one of those. She's so cute!

Willie: You can't have her. You'll have to get your own. [*matter-of-factly*]

Saleswoman: Willie dear, don't make her feel bad. [*to Donna*] Sorry about him.

Donna: Well thank you so much. We had better get home.

In foyer, exiting.

DONNA: Angel, I know it was just a mistake, but you know you shouldn't have asked for the boy's ferret.

Pattern 5. Thinking in words

Symbols are not just for communication; they are also the fundamental units of thought for people with the pattern of *thinking in words*. Some philosophers have suggested that words co-arise with conscious thought, and that without the word there is no thought. Some autistics have been noted to "think in pictures," and thinking in words is the common NT alternative to thinking in pictures (or in other ways).

When thinking in words, **the words mean more than what they mean**, which is to say, their literal meaning is only one part of their full meaning. Going back to definitions, recall that the symbol is composed of a signifier (word) and a signified (what it means). When thinking in words, the signifier also means something; the person develops an emotional connection to the word, or they use the word because they like the word, or because it sounds good.

Here is a statement I once heard that will be analyzed for a basic example: "Our classes start in June and run for a full calendar year." The phrase "calendar year" usually indicates the year starting on January first, as opposed to an academic year, a fiscal year or some other year, which could start on some other day. Omitting the word "calendar" from the statement, the statement would have meant that the year runs from June through the following May. With the word "calendar," it was ambiguous to me: Does it mean June through December of the same year? Why would the speaker say this? My conclusion is that the speaker added the word "calendar" just because it is a word related to "year," and it just seemed to her to fit, but she did not mean to convey a calendar year in any literal sense. So, she was thinking *in* words, or thinking *about* the words, but not necessarily thinking *in terms of the meaning* of the words.

A pattern of thinking in words combined with weak semantics leads to prizing words as ends in themselves. The manipulation of words becomes like an art form, instead of words being used to mean something specific. For example, a hospital has the slogan "We're not just about health - we're about wellness," a phrase suggesting that health and wellness are different, but not indicating what the difference is. This slogan shows the pattern of thinking in words because it avoids facing the meaning, and just relies on the assumption that since the words are different, the meaning must be different.

In the play, the word "essentials" is used without any clear definition, and Donna reacts to it as if she knows what it means. The purpose of the word in relation to the flowers is just to create a distinction between flowers that doesn't actually exist in a literal sense, but can be caused to socially exist by labeling it with a word.

What are the terms of your thought? What is your thinking machine made of and what sorts of terms does it process? (words, pictures, sounds?) I believe I think in signifieds - that is, the things that words refer to, but I think spatially and verbally about signifieds. Understanding and expressing your own way of thinking from within its own limitations can be hard for anyone else to understand.

To examine more about how an NT would use symbols as the units of thought, rather than as the objects of thought, consider the traditional tune "Jingle Bells." Now recall or imagine a modern rendition of that tune, which is highly inflected. If you've ever endured Christmas season in department stores, you've been assaulted with highly inflected traditional carols. Inflected means changed or distorted while still revealing the original thing. When a song or other cultural symbol is inflected, it is shown in its entirety (there is no attempt to hide it) but it is warped or added to by some musical technique. The inflection results in a song that is about the original song, not about what the original song is about. In the case of Jingle Bells, here are three thinkable things:

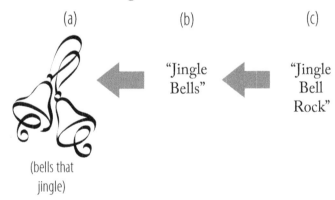

(a)   (b)   (c)

"Jingle Bells"   "Jingle Bell Rock"

(bells that jingle)

Symbols referring to other symbols.

Item (c) points to the item (b) in this diagram. That shows that "Jingle Bell Rock" (the inflected, modern song) is about "Jingle Bells" (the traditional song). The traditional song is about bells, horses, and other physical things. The modern song is not about the actual jingling bells at all. It is about another symbol. It is as if "Jingle Bells" (the words as a symbol) is the part of the brain that is doing the thinking, rather than "Jingle Bells" being the object that is being thought about.

Pattern 6. The belief web

For NTs, words and other symbols are loaded with meanings that go beyond the strict dictionary definition. For example the word "wedding" is loaded with assumptions about who might be there, what it feels like, what you might eat, how long it takes, and so on. If you arrive and there is no minister, no tuxedos, and no wedding cake, you might hear someone say "this is not a wedding!" Or someone might qualify it as a "Jewish wedding" or "hippie wedding" to distinguish it from a "true" (mainstream) wedding in their mind.

The belief web is a generalization of the symbolic web. NT beliefs are symbolic, which is to say NTs generally think and believe in terms of culturally defined symbols.

Another example: the assumption that "Beethoven is great" could exist in the mind of someone who has no personal experience of that greatness, or has not come to that conclusion himself, but has just picked up on the belief in the exact same way that he picked up on the meaning of words as a child by hearing others use them. In that way, "Beethoven is great" becomes a cultural truth that is nearly universally accepted and rarely evaluated.

A vital point in understanding NT behavior is that the belief web is value-laden: there is an emotional affinity or repulsion with each symbol. The values are connected with a person's identity, as explained later. Beliefs are connected to each other through associations. The associations, along with the person's identity, help the person determine whether the beliefs are true or not.

In the play, Star places herself in her belief web close to the idea of "traditional," and uses that association to evaluate whether a certain bouquet is "her" - that is, whether the bouquet is closely associated with her beliefs about herself in her belief web. That's how she determines which flowers would be best for the wedding. Angel has a different set of beliefs about herself that give her affinity to black roses. Even though they are sisters and share the same general culture (the same ethnicity and language), they can have very different internal maps, beliefs and values. Angel is intentionally rebellious in order to differentiate herself from her sister. Donna believes that poinsettias mean something inappropriate, possibly that it is a summer wedding and those flowers are associated with winter. "Inappropriate" in the context of the NT belief web indicates something that does not conform to the web.

If you can step back into autistic space and look at this idea freshly, isn't it remarkable that beliefs can be adopted by association? Can you do this? Can any other species do this? Consider the implications.

Pattern 7. Perception limited to existing beliefs

As mentioned in the topic on perception, **some things have to be believed to be seen**. NTs can have trouble seeing or hearing things that they don't already expect to see or hear, so new ideas can "fall on deaf ears." It is not necessarily the case that they dislike new ideas; they might simply be unable to detect them because of symbolic filtering.

The belief web is used to classify the identity of things in the environment. Raw data comes in and it is filtered into pre-existing categories. If it fits into a category, it is perceived; if not, it may be thrown out as noise.

Some people are more limited to thinking symbolically than others, and cannot perceive and accept the differences between actual reality and their internal categories.

In the play, Angel and Star are constrained by their existing beliefs in their interaction with Willie. The identity (species) of Cinnamon is unknown by the girls, and Willie apparently does not know the species name either. But for Willie, *touching* and *looking at* Cinnamon is sufficient for *knowing* what the pet is. For the older girls, his explanation that "*this* is Cinnamon" is not sufficient for them to *know* Cinnamon, because they insist on knowing the identity (that is, the *name/category*) of the thing, even though they can clearly see and touch the thing. Cinnamon's "is-ness" is more closely determined by the symbolic label it has than by the qualities that it presents to the senses.

Have you ever felt like Willie, trying to explain something that is so obvious to you, and yet the other person can't understand it simply because you aren't feeding them the specific *word* that they need to hear? It may be that they would need the category in their belief web to be mentally constructed through associations first, before they can hear your idea.

Pattern 8. Social reality

A reminder of background theory: Language and culture are socially constructed. Each symbol is both created and shared in the act of communication. It is *during* the communication about things when things develop names.

The *social reality* pattern is the extension of this theory of social construction into the realm of truth and reality. In its strongest form, the person cannot differentiate between consensus opinion and reality, and he apparently has few independent thoughts derived from his own experience, and instead assumes that the only thing that is true is what is communicated.

For NTs with a strong social reality pattern, the truth is not the conclusion drawn from evidence. It is socially constructed. Everything can be socially constructed, even if it is apparently natural. Take a rabbit. A rabbit occurs in nature, yet the somewhat arbitrary line that taxonomists draw, which distinguishes a rabbit from related taxa, creates the mental rabbit. The rabbit *symbol* is a category for all actual rabbits. On the other hand, there are weddings, which do not occur in nature, and are more clearly socially constructed. Yet NTs may think of the rabbit and the wedding in the same way, as things having the same kind of being.

Another example is in the story of the "planet" Pluto. Pluto was recently re-categorized from a planet to a different type of orbiting body, and of course there were no changes on Pluto itself on account of the change of name. However, there were actual marches held in protest about the new status. Some NTs apparently felt they were losing a planet that was dear to their hearts. For those people, the socially constructed name and categorization of the rock is more "reality" than the rock itself, or they cannot differentiate between the name (which exists in their belief web in their minds) and the actual rock (which exists very far away).

In the play, the assertion is made that red and purple are in fashion this year. In that statement, the word "are" designates a real fact, in this pattern of thought. In the NT mind, highly arbitrary and temporary social "reality" can be just as real as natural reality. If someone else makes the case that red is *not* "in" this year, that could be interpreted as an argument over facts, not over preferences.

Another way the play reveals social reality is when Donna corrects Angel after Angel makes a "mistake." The mistake is poor social judgment: Willie might have thought that Angel was going to take his ferret, and Angel was the cause of *potentially* hurt feelings - which is considered a mistake even though Willie's feelings were not *actually* hurt. This type of poor judgment is taken as the same type of poor judgment as something having natural consequences. For example, running on ice could *potentially* result in broken bones, and would be considered a mistake even if no bones were *actually* broken. Having socially hurt feelings is considered just as hard and painful as falling on ice, so making statements that have the potential to hurt feelings are just as much of a mistake regardless of the actual outcome.

An autistic person may be said to be out of touch with the "real world," and in this case, "real" is the NT term for socially constructed reality. If you are autistic, and you hear the phrase "real world," you may need to do some silent translation to understand them.

Where is your reality - nature, feelings, intimacy? For most NTs, socially constructed language and culture is very seriously real, and high-stakes. Success in school and careers depends on it

Scene 3 of The Lockstep Tragedy

At the Whiting house a few days later, the day before the wedding. Antonio is Donna's husband. Valerie is Star's best friend. Ivan is her fiance. Star, Angel and Donna are in the kitchen.

VALERIE: [*enters*] Hey guys. Did you change the flowers?

STAR: I don't know, not really. I guess I was afraid to change anything. I don't know. [*withdrawn*]

IVAN: Valerie's here! All right! We need the excitement.

VALERIE: Hey Ivan. Cheer up, Starling, you'll be great. You should listen to your mom.

STAR: Yeah, um, for the music, did you get the wedding bells cut, the ta da da daa ding ding one I wanted? My idea was probably too dumb.

VALERIE: That music is new age. You want this to be romantic. [*excited*] I was thinking: Each bouquet has to have a ribbon all the way down like this. And he's going to take you right back there [*motions to back yard*] and it will look so pretty. [*dancing around room*] Then the music, and *that's* what romantic is, and that's how you want to remember it, so get out of your puddle of tears honey.

STAR: I thought the bells music was romantic.

IVAN: You could use a clue sometimes; I mean, it's great music though.

STAR: Thanks, little I-dog. [*Star refers to Ivan as her I-dog, short for seeing eye dog.*] I don't know anything.

IVAN: I love you, honey.

Tony enters.

VALERIE: [*to Ivan*] You ready for the big fun day?

TONY: [*to Ivan*] But more importantly, are you ready to keep this family's honor, because you are going to be one of us. That's your job now, buddy. [*lightly punches Ivan*]

DONNA: Oh Tony, he's already one of us, aren't you? Star is a lucky girl.

IVAN: Thanks, but really I'm the lucky one. [*politely*]

DONNA: We're all related, and you can come to me for anything.

Tony: I'm sure as hell not related to your cousin! When that guy gets anywhere near a bar, good *night!* Did you see him last year, trying to shoot baskets? That was hilarious. Me and Paul kept handing him drinks and he goes to the driveway and tries to shoot and the ball keeps going into the trees.

Valerie: Sounds charming.

Angel: Oh yeah and he has that hideous pickup which is always full of beer.

Donna: He's not a drunk and his pickup is just fine. He's my cousin.

Angel: He's been drunk every time I've seen him. Just saying.

Donna: Angel, this is your family, and you *will* be nice at the wedding.

Doorbell rings.

Star: I'll escape - I mean, I'll get the door.

Star goes to the door followed by Valerie.

Star: Hello?

James: [*holding a clipboard*] 321 Broken Arrow?

Star: Yeah...

James: We have a demo tomorrow. Didn't know the house was occupied.

Valerie: [*taking over*] What are you demonstrating? I might be interested.

James: A *demolition.* It's a wrecking business. There should have been a notice. You both live here?

VALERIE: She does. Her wedding is tomorrow. Wanna come?

STAR: Shut up, Val!

JAMES: I could probably squeeze you … in. Ha! Your name is Val? I'm surprised *you're* not married yet.

VALERIE: You watch out, you devil! You're embarrassing the bride.

JAMES: Don't want that. Well, see you round. That was your notice, by the way. And I'm James. [*jogs away*]

VALERIE: Eee! He's so cute! [*jumping*] Can I invite him?

STAR: What the hell are you doing? You have a boyfriend.

VALERIE: I'm just playing. What's the demolition anyway?

STAR: [*serious*] I can NOT handle this concept today. He couldn't have really meant tomorrow. I'm just going to say that he was making that up to get your attention, you little tramp. If you weren't always showing off your big boobs, stuff like this would never happen.

Pattern 9. Free-floating symbols

A symbol may be just a **free-floating cultural symbol**, which is purely socially constructed, and not a label for any specific thing. Names of styles like "Victorian" or "gourmet" are good examples. They are much more than their dictionary definitions; in fact

NTs usually won't even be able to agree on what the definition is. They are self-identifying globs of feelings, environments, and attitudes. There is no sensory evidence that can corroborate free-floating cultural symbols, so these only exist by being communicated; they are created in the retelling.

As a reminder, the illustration of the symbol of the rabbit is repeated below, showing that the word points to something in nature.

rabbit ➡
signifier   signified

A symbol that points to something in nature.

For a free-floating symbol, there is no signified:

gourmet ➡ **?**

A symbol that does not point to anything in nature.

So, why is there a word if it doesn't mean anything? It does mean something, associatively. That means it has connections to other symbols, but it is not a sign that stands for a particular signified.

NT adults use their senses *to some degree* to collect evidence about the world around them, and weigh what they see against their prior belief. But for free-floating symbols, they cannot use their own senses to verify a belief, so the belief is both created and verified by communicating it.

I've always been a person who uses words only to mean specific things that I understand, and for most of my life, when I heard NTs using free-floating symbols, I didn't know what they meant, and I thought they knew something that I didn't know. But as it turns out, they only knew things in a different way - an associative way, but they did not know the meaning of the symbols in the literal way as I had thought.

In the play, Valerie defines "romantic" as a constellation of concepts, including the groom taking the bride to a certain place in a story-book-like reenactment, pretty things including ribbons and bouquets of flowers, and music. Those are just a few of the ideas associated with the concept of romantic. How did Valerie learn what all those associations are so she can be so sure of what it means? Valerie spends a great deal of time exchanging symbolic information with others, so this kind of thing probably came from her friends and family. In this scene, she is revealing her symbolic web explicitly, and the others are sitting around listening and retaining that associative information.

Pattern 10. Liquid truth

One of the NT strategies for handling ambiguity is to believe something *part way*, like a cup partly full of water. If the level is low, it is believed only a little, and if high, it is believed a lot. This "liquid truth" can be highly dynamic, and depends on the moment by moment connection between the belief in question and a number of related beliefs.

Here's a piece of a belief web:

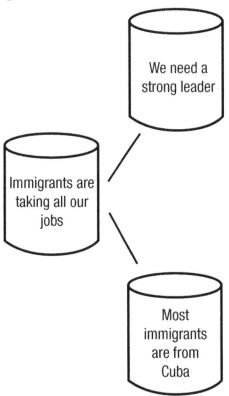

Some propositions in a belief web,
shown as cups of water.

The "truth" in liquid truth is not to be confused with literal measurable truth. It is the amount of affinity a person has with an idea, or the strength of association between the idea under consideration and the person's idea of herself. There is an emotional element to the adherence to the "truth." Also, don't confuse liquid truth with things that are simply unknown. For example, I don't know if my cousin's cat is still living because I haven't asked her lately; I have no particular belief about that. Liquid truth comes into play concerning beliefs that are less subject to readily available evidence and more socially constructed.

For individuals living with the liquid truth pattern, things commonly "sort-of are" and "sort-of aren't" at the same time. Beliefs have many associations connecting to other beliefs, so they are being pulled in different directions. Picture the associations as chains pulling on the beliefs.

A person might believe that "the Eiffel Tower is THE place to go in Paris," but the proposition is dynamic and the statement has a less than 100% truth to it; it's a liquid belief that could change. There are chains pulling it towards true and chains pulling it towards false. Some chains are heavier than others, and the heaviest chains determine the overall amount of belief in the proposition. The weights of the chains depend on the truth of the connected beliefs, which in turn depend on who believes them and who the person wants to be, as will be covered later.

Suppose a person P has a half-full cup of truth about the Eiffel tower, and he meets up with person A, who claims convincingly that "the Eiffel Tower is

THE place to go," it would fill the cup and make it more true. But if he met up with person B, who claims "the Eiffel Tower is just where dumb tourists go," P could instantly change his level of liquid belief to a low level, to avoid a self association with dumb tourists.

Here is a picture of how the value of the Eiffel Tower can be manipulated by chains of associations. This analogy is only meant to give you a picture of the liquidity of beliefs.

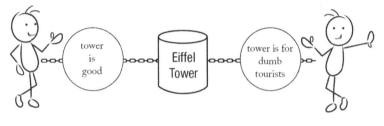

Person A   Person B

People pulling the truth value of a proposition in different ways by pulling on it with chains of associations to other beliefs.

In the play, Star holds the belief that poinsettias are possibly good flowers for a wedding, but Donna confidently dismisses that belief on unspoken grounds. It can be surmised that Star's level of belief is changed by having the association with a negative reputation. Later, she makes a similar choice for a "new age" piece of music which is unpopular with the others, and changes her belief in that.

Donna's cousin's pickup is considered by Angel to be "hideous," probably because of its association with the person and his drinking. If the same truck were owned by someone else, it might be perceived differently. Donna can't accept the judgment about the cousin because of the association between him and herself. Whether he *actually* is drunk every time Angel has seen him is not what is being discussed. Donna is saying that he was not drunk and that the pickup is not hideous, in order to protect the associations, not in order to make points about those things. If she were to admit he was drunk, the chain of associations would devalue herself.

The important thing about the discussion of the cousin is that they are *not* primarily talking about the facts; that was just a starting point. They are exchanging a whole web of beliefs, all of which affect the level of truth of the original proposition.

I've made the mistake many times of believing I was in a conversation with NTs about the things that were being mentioned in the conversation. What was actually happening is that they were making claims about things in order to protect unspoken associated liquid truths. When Donna says "the truck is *not* hideous," she is not even talking about the truck. She is saying that her cousin should not be de-valued by association with anything labeled hideous.

Have you ever been confused because conversation wasn't really about what was being said?

Pattern 11. Lumping

Words with their collections of loaded meanings become one inseparable ball of wax, with a single name. For example, at a public meeting on road construction, I heard someone say they wanted to remove the orange barrels. I first thought that their proposal was to do the construction project without the use of the protective orange barrels, which I thought would be foolish. As I learned later, the person was referring to the entire construction site as "orange barrels," and by asking to remove the barrels, was indirectly asking to cancel the whole construction job.

Lumping is a term for the "ball of wax" that combines potentially separate ideas into one, and this ties together the linguistic theory of perceiving in symbols with the theory of belief being liquid and connected by chains to other beliefs. Another way to consider lumping is the confusion between the map and the territory.

Take this scenario: Person A was found with her hand on B's neck and B was dead. Possibly A was checking B's pulse on the neck. But an assumption that the NT mind might draw from the scenario is that A killed B - depending on many factors. An observer might even say "I *know* that A killed B." The liquid belief of the event did not come from perception; it came from chaining to other beliefs, such as the character and motivation of A.

This scenario illustrates the saying "where there's smoke, there's fire," which in this case means: where there is indirect evidence of an event, then the event must have happened. The NT mind is also capable of lumping the smoke and fire into one thing. For example, an observer might say "Even if she was just checking the pulse, she should have known that it would *look* suspicious, so it was wrong to do that." In other words, things are what they appear. The NT mind is often not good at distinguishing appearances from the facts that underlie those appearances. To appear to do good is doing good. To claim that one is supportive is the same as being supportive.

Sometimes a word in a phrase will define the meaning of a phrase because of its individual associations, regardless of the context of the phrase. Here's a strange but true story: several people in a church were vehemently opposed to adopting "goals for the long range building plan" but were fine with adopting "long range goals for the building." The word "plan" was lumped for them with some negative feelings, and those negative associations made anything containing the word "plan" feel negative. They could not peel apart the words from the other things in the ball of wax. By changing the wording in a way that did *not* substantially change the referential meaning, but *did* change the associative meaning, the opponents became supporters.

Other cases of lumping are:

• lumping sex (natural body traits) with gender (culturally learned traits).

• lumping of a case (something happened once), a statistic (something happens most of the time), and a universal (something always happens)

• lumping of motivation, behavior, and appearance of behavior

Scene 4 of The Lockstep Tragedy

Paul Lineman's house. Paul is Ivan's father and Tony's best friend. Paul's girlfriend Carmen Fast is there. Star and Ivan enter.

Iᴠᴀɴ: [*airily*] Hi Dad. [*flatly*] Hello Carmen.

CARMEN: This must be Star? Hello hello! I've been wanting to meet you. You must be so excited for your wedding tomorrow! The weather is supposed to be wonderful.

STAR: Didn't we meet? [*confused, she remembers seeing her in scene 1*]

CARMEN: I'm Carmen, so nice to meet you. I was just discussing the real estate boom with Paul. He likes my idea so I'm *on it* like a bug on water. I'm going to make my fortune on townhouses. Maybe *we'll* even get married too.

PAUL: I'm not sure if it is appropriate to be discussing that right now. Let's sit down.

CARMEN: Just an option, hun. [*cheerily*] Anything can happen!

All sit down.

IVAN: [*stiffly*] Anything can happen... So how do you make a fortune on townhouses?

CARMEN: Townhouses are the future, for sure. [*Star remembers where she saw Carmen.*] You have to be at the right place at the right time and make a few sweet deals. I have people, but you wouldn't understand that.

IVAN: Townhouses, hm... I'd hate to be watching a game and it's tied at the bottom of the ninth, and the neighbors are all yelling and banging on the walls.

STAR: [*absently*] I know.

IVAN: Do you buy them or rent them?

CARMEN: Oh yes, people buy them, definitely. They are not like apartments [*hand motion indicating disgust*] - it's a whole entire house for you, a townhouse. I'm just now getting into it. They rent them out too, more like a lease I guess. It would be perfect for you and Star. Are you planning children?

STAR: There seems to be one on the way. [*Everyone but Carmen already knows.*]

CARMEN: That's nice.

IVAN: Star, we should get one, you know, a townhouse.

CARMEN: You could be the first. I have two old properties on Broken Arrow, and they are going down tomorrow, and that's where my first row is going up.

IVAN: That's where Star's folks live. I hope it isn't too close to them.

CARMEN: I have a great guy. He's going to take them down tomorrow and the surveyors are coming Monday. You gotta be fast and furious!

PAUL: Maybe that's enough on that.

Pause. Star makes the connection to James.

STAR: This isn't happening.

IVAN: Jittery? Everything will be fine when it's all over. [*referring to the wedding*] I love you.

STAR: [*quietly and weakly*] I love you, I-dog. You will take care of everything?

IVAN: Sure.

PAUL: It's normal to feel anxious. Maybe you two need some rest apart from each other. And I promised Donna I'd have the shirts ready for your little cousins. Can you find out what she needs?

Ivan: Sure.

Carmen: Won't that be nice.

Star whispers to Ivan.

Ivan: [*afraid*] Um, Miss Carmen? That's not 321 Broken Arrow by any chance.

Carmen: My properties? [*agitated*] They are vacant, if that's what you are asking. I was assured they will be vacant. Why do you need to know all this?

Ivan: Of course, nothing. Um, I'm sure you've seen the address on the wedding invitation. I don't want to cause a problem, but -

Carmen: I'm not really family, though I appreciate the thought. [*a forced smile*] You wouldn't want me there I'm sure. And I have business to take care of.

Paul: [*with authority*] I think what Carmen is trying to say, is that she wishes the best for your wedding, as do I. Rest is the key at this point. You are both very anxious I can see.

Pattern 12. Attrition

For NTs, truth leaks. As an analogy, the cups of water making up liquid beliefs have small holes, and the beliefs are always gradually leaking out. Any kind of belief of fact (or value or attitude) is constantly undergoing attrition, in the absence of being refilled. For example, an NT loves her husband and says "I love you," which slightly refills their cups of belief in that proposition. By repeating it frequently, it keeps the statement true. By failing to repeat it, the statement undergoes attrition (leaking) and eventually becomes false. In the play, Ivan and Star remind each other that they still love each other, not because of any specific evidence to the contrary, but just to counter the natural tendency of attrition.

People with pronounced attrition patterns must constantly interact and repeat things to each other because it maintains the internal mental map of the shared culture; symbols come and go and change their position within the symbolic web through repetition.

The topics that are most prone to rapid attrition are those that are the free-floating socially constructed symbols.

The phenomenon of attrition explains why NTs are often excellent at adapting to new environments. Old beliefs and patterns become obsolete and slip away, making room for new beliefs and patterns. The NT mind is very dynamic in that sense. By contrast, autistics tend to believe something permanently or until there is evidence to the contrary, and are often poor at adapting or accepting to social change.

Their adaptability makes NTs responsive to advertising and propaganda. NTs can be swept up in a new belief or in brand loyalty, even one that is very destructive, without being able to independently assess its value.

Have you ever found that some plan or understanding just disappeared over time, when no formal mention was ever made? Have you been accused of hanging on to things that are no longer relevant to others?

Pattern 13. Forest-first learning

Areas of understanding can often be viewed both in a general holistic way - the forest - and in a detailed way - the trees. The expression "not seeing the forest for the trees" refers to looking exclusively at details and missing the big picture.

The pattern of **forest-first learning** refers to learning about a subject in a gradual holistic way. In the upper sequence in the following diagrams, we see first the vague notion of a forest, then a definite forest, and finally the forest composed of trees. A "little bit of everything" becomes revealed, then a bit more of everything.

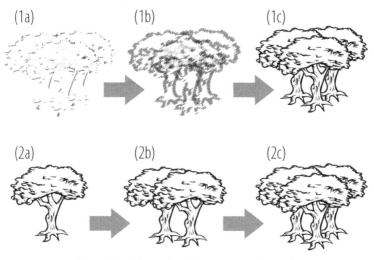

Forest-first learning (top sequence), and trees-first learning (bottom sequence) show that two different ways of learning lead to the same result.

The alternative way of learning, shown in the lower sequence, is to get to know one tree at a time, and then after knowing about enough individual trees (details), realizing that they compose a forest.

This way (trees-first learning) appears to be more common to autistics, and we use it to build independent mental maps. The "forests" that are built in a trees-first way are more independently known, while the "forests" that are communicated and learned in a forest-first way are cultural symbols, and are therefore understood in more similar ways by a group.

As a person who relies on trees-first learning, I have fragmented awareness while learning something: "I know that I only know part of what I need to know." But during forest-first learning, the NT can have the illusion of full awareness. The NT might fail to adjust the big picture to the current actual contents of the details, and might create an inaccurate conclusion.

In the play, Carmen gives the impression of knowing all about developing townhouses, but when questioned, she reveals that she doesn't know many of the details. She just knows the whole feeling of it. The important thing for her about the question of renting versus buying is to distance what she's doing from apartments, which she apparently considers lower class. In order to create the distance in the mental map, she states unequivocally that they must be bought, like a house, not rented. After stating that, she states that they can be rented too. The actual details (trees) are clearly of much less concern to her than the townhouses as a symbol of progress or social class (the forest).

Forest-first learning does not depend on being observant of each detail. The details can feel irrelevant or detracting from the whole. A forest-first person will see the whole as not only *more than* the sum of the parts, but also *separate* from the parts. (By contrast, a trees-first person will see the whole as just another name for the sum of the parts.)

In a scientific or historical study, forest-first learning could contribute to the error of starting with the desired conclusion, and filling in the details that allegedly support the conclusion.

Pattern 14. Certainty

If you ask a young NT who has heard the word "gourmet" only a few times (or any other free-floating symbol), "what does 'gourmet' mean?," she might claim that she is very *certain* what it means, and then go on to fumble with words and give a nonsensical definition. In the learning process, NT's make mental chains between the thing and other symbols, and even if there are just a few chains, that is enough to place the thing in the symbolic web. So, 'gourmet' might be chained to some other concepts like unusual food served with heavy cloth napkins and parsley that you are not supposed to actually eat. Or she may have other associations. When the certainty pattern applies, at the beginning, a person will say she "knows" what it means, even if it is only the vaguest notion. As she is exposed to an idea repeatedly, the chains increase and the position of the thing in the web adjusts towards more accuracy.

Have you felt uncertain when you are around people who appear to be certain? They may not know more than you, but their way of thinking is more certain.

Certainty about what a thing is comes from the conviction that it is placed *somewhere* in the symbolic web. It is not based on the amount of exposure.

Such people therefore live life *as if* what they know is known perfectly. They report being sure about most things. At the same time, they are not stuck on their particular incomplete knowledge; they allow it to change fluidly.

In autism circles, the term "weak central coherence" refers to the opposite of certainty about the big picture, or the theory that autistic people have trouble seeing the big picture. A more positive view of weak central coherence is the accurate reporting of how well a subject is understood in its entirety.

Examine this series of addition problems:

$$2 + \_ + \_ + \_ = ?$$
$$2 + 8 + \_ + \_ = ?$$
$$2 + 8 + 5 + \_ = ?$$
$$2 + 8 + 5 + 1 = ?$$

If you were to ask *me* these four problems in a row as questions, I would give these four answers: *"I don't know," "I don't know," "I don't know," "16."* Certainty does not increase at all until the fourth problem, at which time it jumps from 0% certainty to 100% certainty. There simply is no big picture at all until it is fully painted. That's also my way of learning everything else. So if you were to ask me what "gourmet" means, I would also say "I don't know" since I don't have a complete idea of that word. There is at least one blank in my understanding (like the blanks in the addition formulas), so the answer is not known.

The addition problems are just an analogy for social knowledge. What I notice about NTs is that they know things even if the things have blanks in them. They still report being certain, to some degree. In the four addition problems above, an NT might feel increasingly certain as more blanks are filled with numbers. Of course this logic does not hold mathematically, but as an analogy to social knowledge, the idea is that partial knowledge is enough to give partial certainty.

Going back to the liquid truth pattern, you may notice a discrepancy in how I explained certainty and how I explained the "sort-of true, sort-of false" quality of liquid truth. The liquid truth pattern does not result in NTs acting hesitantly and ambivalently. They may be very sure of a belief, but the liquidity of it means they could flip flop to the opposite belief suddenly.

In the play, Carmen says "people buy them, definitely" when she doesn't really have the basis for that level of certainty.

Pattern 15. Social learning

New information and beliefs can be learned by NTs socially - that is, by hearing someone else say it, or reading it, as opposed to perceiving or experiencing it.

The source of new information and beliefs often comes from an **authority**, whether it is the dominant cultural authority or some counter-cultural authority. For example, it could come from a parent, scientists, the mayor, a popular singer, or anyone that has a following. The authority status of the sender affects whether the receiver will accept or reject the new information.

People with a strong social learning pattern can have difficulty having an independent thought or coming to a conclusion through logic. They tend not to believe themselves. When presented with new sensory information, if it is not seeable through the symbolic filter, it may be ignored altogether. If it is not connected to an authority, it may be dismissed.

Have you tried to tell someone something, but were dismissed, even though you were sure it was correct? Maybe you were not perceived as an authority by the other person; therefore they could not easily learn from you.

Pattern 16. Lockstep learning

In the lockstep pattern, learning occurs in lockstep with others. This is a group pattern. Often, NTs don't like to believe things outside of their group, so the whole group has to learn at once in many small steps. Learning in a way that everyone involved learns at the same rate can make learning slow. So, while NT individuals can be very flexible and adaptable as they change from one group or environment to another, the groups themselves are much slower at learning.

An alternate word with a slightly different analogy is a gridlock. In gridlocked traffic, no single car can solve the problem; it has to be loosened up gradually by many small movements.

*Marching band in lockstep. No one can get ahead
when all are marching to the same drummer.*

A very basic example of lockstep learning is how large groups like government learn to adopt a more advantageous position. Suppose you have discovered a way for the government to save a large amount of money. Simply dropping them a note explaining the technique will not be enough to set the change in motion, because the people reading the note generally cannot or will not learn from an outsider having no authority, and especially not when that learning would put them at odds with their peers. The NTs in government would have to wait until many others were also ready to learn the new technique, then they would all take the step together, very slowly in lockstep.

In a series of meetings to look at a new plan, such as a plan for roads, public parks, or other city improvements, the default position of the group is to make no change, or at least not give up anything. Someone with an alternate view might introduce it as a "thought experiment" or "just brainstorming" and it might be dismissed as radical or funny. After many people have made references to the idea, which could take years, it might be considered either as a realistic option, or as a threat. There could be conferences with invited speakers to go over the idea repeatedly. It can be a very long process between introducing a new idea and having it adopted.

In lockstep groups, some people may contribute to the slow learning because they are social learners, and thus cannot internalize a belief unless it is already a socially dominant belief. They just take a "wait and see" attitude about most things and strive to stick only to dominant beliefs. Others may not rely solely on social learning, but they may have other limitations.

In the play, you could argue that the characters should have discovered and investigated the error - that the house was scheduled for demolition on the wedding day - and calmly run through some options and settled on a plan that would eliminate the conflict. But what happens in the play is that the limitations of each character conspire to keep any reasonable resolution from being enacted.

Pattern 17. Holistic training

To explain the holistic training pattern, I'm going to simplify things by contrasting two patterns, and calling them holistic (the pattern of NTs) and autistic. Not everyone fits neatly into one pattern, of course.

Holistic trainees learn holistically (in a totality), learning a little of the whole, then another little of the whole and so on. For example, if the training is for a job as a cashier, the NT would need to get used to the idea of the job gradually, then fill in details. They would get the rhythm of it, and follow the lead of the trainer. He might adopt the language and attitude of the trainer, then *later* understand details, such as the fact that the register is calculating tax. It would be nearly impossible to fully communicate the detail of the tax calculation until *after* the trainee has gotten accustomed to the general aspects of the job.

This is a forest-first learning style: First the forest as a whole, then gradually learn how the forest is made of trees.

By contrast, the *autistic* pattern is trees-first: learning that the register adds up prices, calculates tax, and so on, then putting together all the detailed requirements of the job into a total performance of the job.

With the holistic learning style, learning can occur out of order, or without any particular structure. Things that are more fundamental don't have to be learned first; derived ideas can be learned, and the the ideas that they rest on can be filled in later. The internal structure is a symbolic web that has no superstructure. As long as new information can be attached somewhere to the web, it can be learned and retained. For example, an holistic type can often remember dates in history (1492, 1812) where each isolated fact has its own significance, without first having to know a more fundamental structure (such as eras in history) on which to pin dates. Going back to the cashier example, the person could learn a vague idea of the tax calculation, then learn other things, then cycle back and firm up the understanding of the tax.

Holistic trainees might need extended job training over a substantial period of time, even if they are very intelligent. Without a superstructure of thinking, they must adapt in lockstep, which can be slow. They may only be sure they know the job when they know others know they know the job.

Have you been trained in a holistic way and felt you didn't understand it, or that you were expected to get it sooner? Perhaps you weren't given enough details on which to build your own structure of understanding. Have you had to train someone else and felt a mismatch between your way of teaching and the way they need to learn?

Pattern 18. Mapping between time and space

Language is temporal (relating to time) and doesn't occupy space, but words create a correspondence between time and space. Although the specifics probably vary by culture, the common American mental map is that language is a continuously moving queue that is coming at the receiver. Therefore, saying "A is in front of B" is saying A arrives first in time, or is before B. "I'll push my meeting back," means I'll push my meeting further away from me, so it gets to me later on.

To my mind, references to "in front of" and "behind" referring to words or schedules was always nonsensical (and I had to ask them to put it in different terms), until I figured out there was a cultural pattern mapping space and time.

Pattern 19. Going through the motions

In the pattern of going through the motions, the person continues to do residual procedures when the original need for them is no longer present. The actions have been divorced from their original meaning. In lockstep with others, they *gradually* learn to stop doing the residual procedure.

Technology changes are some of the simplest examples of this pattern. For example, telegrams are obsolete in every technical respect, but can still be sent. If people have meaningful memories of sending or receiving a telegram for a funeral (which was at one time common), they may still want to re-enact the obsolete technology.

In my software business, I have often designed software to make previous procedures unnecessary, because the whole purpose of investing in custom software is to streamline operations. However in some cases, users will just add the new software's procedures to the old procedures and have trouble letting go of the old.

Autistic people don't take advantage of culturally-prescribed ways of doing things as much as NTs do, so some comparisons can help shed light on what "going through the motions" really means mentally.

- In an emergency situation that has never happened before to the people involved, it's often noted that autistics can rise to the occasion - for us, it isn't that much different than day to day situations, which can feel like completely new situations all the time. Some of us can think from general principles to specific actions quickly, while some NTs can become mentally paralyzed for lack of a known procedure.

- In a work situation where procedures are gradually shaped and stray from the original intent based on informal arrangements between co-workers, NTs will adapt, while autistics might fail to notice the change or insist on the official procedure.

- In a work situation where procedures are abruptly replaced (for example, by new management), autistics can be more likely to change and let go of the old, while NTs can resist and continue to go through the motions of the old procedures.

In all these cases, the NTs are learning in lockstep, through social communication, which can be slower but is more adaptive.

Recap

The NT patterns of belief and learning are based on the concept of the belief web - an extension of the symbolic web. The belief web is a web of associations connecting concepts, beliefs, and other propositions (which may be believed or disbelieved). Thinking for NTs is symbolic, which is to say NTs commonly think in words as the basic unit of thought.

Because of their symbolic thinking, they often can't distinguish between natural and social reality, they lump things together by association into an inseparable "ball of wax," and they may only perceive things that they are already aware of a category for. They create free-floating symbols (created in the retelling) that have no literal meaning, but only associative meaning; that is, they only mean what they are associated with in the web. The belief web is constantly being reshaped - each belief is liquid and can be filled or emptied by its associations, or drained gradually through attrition.

Learning is often forest-first, a gradual holistic type of learning. Things feel certain to them even if they don't have many of the details. Groups of NTs keep their learning synchronized in lockstep.

A more general recap

So far the book has discussed:

- *language and culture* - the categories of the mind to chop up the world into communicable bits

- *perception* - the world moving into the mind

- *belief and learning* - the construction of the world in the mind

We have gotten through the psychology of the individual NT in isolation, and are about to embark on the psychology of the NT relating to others.

The following sections will discuss:

- *communication* - moving bits of beliefs from one mind to another's mind

- *feelings and display* - the making of the self as one of the communicable bits

- *relationships and power* - the force of the self with or against others

The book's series of patterns will culminate with sex and socializing, which are among the most complex achievements of the species. I would love for you to pause and consider the six bullet points above, and especially to consider how they build on each other from a foundation (language) all the way up to a peak (relationships).

Patterns of Communication

The patterns in this chapter explain how NTs are able to share the culture and build on the shared culture through intense and frequent communication. In the next scene of the play, a lot of pointless-sounding communication happens, showing ways NTs communicate for reasons other than to convey information.

Scene 5 of The Lockstep Tragedy

Saturday at the Whiting's house. Guests are arriving for the wedding. Paul approaches Tony and Donna.

Donna: Hello Paul! That suit looks sharp.

Paul: It seemed fitting. And you look wonderful, Donna. Nice to see you too, Tony.

Tony: Welcome, my old friend. [*stretches out arms as if to hug, but doesn't*] Here we are. Seeing you here reminds me of our high school buddies. And that reminds me of high school - now where's the booze?

Donna: [*turns to Tony with wide eyes*] Tony!

Paul: [*teasing*] Never too early for you, huh?

Tony: Nah, we'll save it for later. Haven't seen the minister yet. Nice day though.

Donna: Couldn't ask for better weather. We can thank Him for that. [*looks up*]

Paul: You got that right. It was breezy earlier but that seems to have died down.

Donna: Well I hope it doesn't kick up again.

Tony: It should stay pretty nice. Y'all wait here. There's the minister's car. [*exits*]

Donna: Oh, he has one of those minis.

Paul: They sell a lot of them now.

Donna: I pictured him in a pickup. He reminds me of a ranger guy.

Paul: He's sure got that back woods look. [*forced laugh*]

Donna: Paul, have you met Valerie? [*draws in Valerie, followed by Angel*] She's helping with the food and everything.

Paul: I have not had the honor. Are you a relative of Star's?

Donna exits.

Valerie: We're friends. We've been joined at the hip since we were in kindergarten. I'm Valerie, and you?

PAUL: I'm Ivan's father. I'm Paul Lineman.

VALERIE: Hi. [*turning to Angel*] Hey Angel-cakes, what a doll you are. Are you helping me get Star ready?

ANGEL: I thought she had left me for dead. [*eyes downcast*]

VALERIE: Come on, it will be fun. I'll get you ready too. [*caresses Angel and smiles*]

We turn to another conversation in progress, with Tony, Donna, and Ivan.

IVAN: Miss Donna, um, thank you again for you know, the house and everything you've done. You are so helpful!

DONNA: Oh, that's sweet of you. I'd do it all over again.

TONY: Again? Do you know how much we put out for this? [*Ivan stares.*] Heh, just kidding, boy. When you're financially responsible [*indicating himself*] you can *provide.* We're in fine shape of course. You know what the secret to success is?

IVAN: No sir, what?

TONY: The secret is to *provide.* That puts you in charge. When you're the one paying the bills, then what?

IVAN: Well, that's responsibility? [*guessing*]

TONY: I'll tell you what. Calling the shots. You can call the shots. When you can provide, you're the boss. Remember that. If you want to call the shots, you need to be the one paying the bills, and that's where the money comes in, if you know what I mean.

ANGEL: [*entering, to Ivan*] That would be great if we had any money which we don't... not that you care.

IVAN: I wouldn't have let you put out so much if I had known it was a problem.

Donna looks at Angel directly with hands on hips. Angel cocks her head and rolls her eyes.

DONNA: What I have to put up with!

Angel bolts. Paul enters.

TONY: [*to Paul*] We're a good family, my friend. I don't think your boy understands that.

IVAN: I should probably get ready.

TONY: [*to Ivan*] Do you think we're poor folk? What, do you think we're bums?

IVAN: No sir.

PAUL: [*to Tony*] What are you onto him for? This is neither the time nor the place.

DONNA: Yes, *I* need to get some things ready too.

TONY: You'll stay right here until I'm done explaining. I'm done now, so you all run along and have a good time.

Donna and Ivan exit.

Pattern 20. Multi-level communication

NTs communicate - **a lot**. There are many levels of communication:

- Chemistry
- Body language

- Facial expressions
- Words used to convey identity or feelings
- Words used to convey information

It's often said that 80% of communication is nonverbal. Maybe this one of those social facts that is "true" because it is repeated so often. In any case, of the verbal part, only a small amount may be informational.

Consider the two billboards that follow.

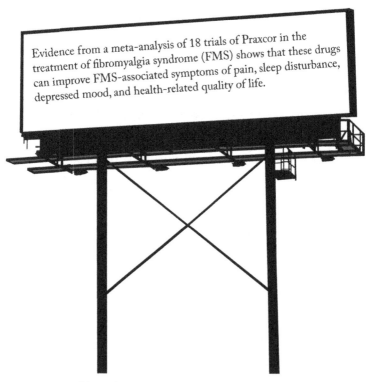

Evidence from a meta-analysis of 18 trials of Praxcor in the treatment of fibromyalgia syndrome (FMS) shows that these drugs can improve FMS-associated symptoms of pain, sleep disturbance, depressed mood, and health-related quality of life.

Billboard containing only the informational

level of communication.

Billboard containing some other levels of communication, but no information,

The second billboard communicates but has no information: Praxcor is a brand name and snumm isn't a word at all. Yet it communicates *more* to NTs than the first billboard. While it does not communicate anything on the level of information, if does communicate on the other levels (body language, expressions, and feelings), which the first one does not.

As a second example, here is a passage from *Little Women*, showing how a lot of communication occurs over a period of time without any words at all:

Jo's face was a study next day, for the secret rather weighed upon her and she found it hard not to look mysterious and important. Meg observed it, but did not trouble herself to make inquiries, for she had learned that the best way to manage Jo was by the law of contraries, so she felt sure of being told everything if she did not ask. She was rather surprised, therefore, when the silence remained unbroken, and Jo assumed a patronizing air, which decidedly aggravated Meg, who in turn assumed an air of dignified reserve, and devoted herself to her mother.

If you were in this situation, would you be attuned to the nonverbal communication, or would you assume that nothing was being communicated, because nothing was being said? Would you recognize a "patronizing air" if you saw one?

If you got no knowledge from the second billboard above, or you wouldn't be likely to pick up on the nonverbal messages in *Little Women*, then it may be hard for you to decipher all the levels of NT's communication in real time.

Pattern 21. Stretching out the message

Any information conveyed in speaking may be stretched out and manipulated in order to also encompass other levels of communication. The amount of time used by an NT to communicate is based on the time needed to give the *nonverbal* message, not the time needed to say the words. Words can be strung together in repetitive and decorated fashion in order to fill that time; the words may have only vague meaning. It is even common for the words to come out with a literal meaning that is incomplete or self contradictory. For example, I heard an educator say something like this once:

> "At this point in time, our kids need a lot more help, and we need to really start to give special emphasis on math and reading, and all the basics, and these things are so important, and also the other subjects as well, and I feel at this time it is important to recognize that all our teachers are doing such a wonderful job in all areas."

Does the person mean that we need to narrow or broaden the focus of education? Do they mean that education is failing, or working very well? All possible interpretations are carefully included in the self-negating statement, because the statement was only uttered to use up the time it took to communicate the nonverbal messages. Ornamentation (such as "at this point in time") is used to increase the time spent communicating.

The educator was communicating, but not much on the literal level. Most of what she was communicating was about drawing associations between beliefs, and supporting other people, and pulling people into the same group with the same emphasis. Here is a more autistic-oriented translation of what she said:

> "All of us are working towards the same purpose. I'm supporting your work. All of us are working towards the same purpose. I'm supporting your work. All of us are working towards the same purpose. I'm supporting your work. All of us are working towards the same purpose. I'm supporting your work."

The repetition is there in the "translation" because it takes longer to give the nonverbal message than it does to give the literal message. The words must expand to fill the time.

In the play, Tony's speech about financial responsibility has only one trivial point stated in the expressed message, but is repetitive and punctuated with questions to Ivan. The nonverbal message given by all the decoration is that Tony is in charge of seemingly everything; that is apparently his wish. All the words are repeated and stretched out in order to give more time for the nonverbal message.

Pattern 22. Influential communication

NT communication quite often has the primary purpose of influencing others or influencing ones own status in a group or identification with a group. The *main* purpose for NTs is rarely to convey information.

The primary messages given in a conversation, if they were to be translated into direct words, would include: "We are in the same group." (or we are in different groups) "I am higher (or lower) than you in rank in our group." These messages reinforce ones identity as a member of a group, and create bonding between people who share a group identity.

The influence isn't always about getting someone to do something, but could be about "making" them feel something - happy, threatened, or guilty, for example. The message is whatever it takes to bring about the desired state of feeling or action in the other person. Sometimes the message is stretched out (see previous pattern). At other times the message could be quite minimal, if that is all it takes to bring about the desired state.

Examples in the play of direct influence include when Donna chastises Tony just by saying "Tony!" when he asks for the booze; when Valerie caresses Angel and smiles and says "Come on!"; and also when Tony tells people what to do directly.

When Tony tells Paul that his son doesn't understand, when Ivan is present, Tony is making a calculated attempt to influence Ivan to feel ashamed, and keep Tony in the more powerful position.

Pattern 23. Small talk

Particularly at the beginning of an NT conversation, the topic selected is often based on whatever is at hand, such as the weather, or some object or event that is immediately present. The parties generally have nothing to say *about* the topic (that is, they had no prior thoughts that needed to be communicated), but a topic is needed to fill out the conversational form and "test the waters."

Small talk can be about trivial or important subjects. (The subject matter is not what defines small talk.) The main rule of small talk is that it must consist of *noncommittal* statements about those subjects. Even during small talk, NTs are very efficient at what they are doing. They are performing a trial run where they reveal their points of manipulation and identity (topics to be covered later in more detail). After the trial run, they can add heavier topics but continue the same conversational form. During small talk, the people are trying to place others (find out their identity) without committing to anything themselves. There is no need to finish a subject, since the subject is not the point of the communication. It doesn't matter that a possibly controversial topic is used; it just matters that whatever is said about it, the speaker cannot be faulted for taking a stand or being controversial. The more inappropriate the topic is, the more can be learned about the other people.

In the play, the weather, the booze, and the minister's car are subjects for small talk. When Tony mentions booze, he intentionally leaves it ambiguous as to whether he is joking or not, in order to find out what is appropriate from someone else. Donna answers that question by indicating it is not appropriate. When Donna talks about the minister's car, she tests the social waters to see if it is appropriate to make judgments about the minister. Since Paul makes a noncommittal joke about it, it is learned that a light judgment of the clergy might be appropriate. But if Paul had said something more formal, it would have communicated that such judgments were off limits.

It is important to understand about NT small talk that it is NOT just wasting time, or "about nothing." If you have tried to mimic it unsuccessfully, it could be that you were actually talking about nothing, and doing nothing else; they would have found you to be dull in that case. Small talk is active discovery.

Pattern 24. Fast, fluid communication

NTs can process all the levels of messages from many sources all at once, and also talk back fluidly. This is possible because they are only processing a small collection of symbols which are extracted from all the levels of messages, and they are only really dealing with the signifier half of the symbol.

Some autistic people wonder how they can process "so many rules" so quickly in order to determine what is the right thing to say at just the right moment. But they are not processing rules; they are just re-hashing their shared symbolic web. Communications are only fluid within a cultural group where the web is shared. The mental web already contains the answers (that is, what to say). So there is no need to "calculate" what is an appropriate thing to say.

In the play, "where's the booze" leads to "never too early" because the time of day when one drinks alcohol is already part of the belief web, and Paul just spits out the closest association that comes to mind. Mention of the minister and the weather leads Donna to think that God is to thank for the weather, and so she says it. Pickups and rangers are associated. A lot of the shifts in topic are based on an association of words, and not on any deeper meaning.

There is very little calculated thought when communication is fast and fluid. If you try to mimic fluid NT communication without memorizing the shared belief web, but you instead try to think it out in real time, you might not be able to do it fast enough.

Pattern 25. Inferring by association

NTs may make inferences based on their internal associations, even if there is no logical basis for the inference. For example: suppose you are speaking to an employee of the World Wildlife Fund (WWF), and you say "Your logo is a panda. I don't like pandas." Those are two independent unrelated statements, at least on the literal level. But an NT listener would probably infer that you don't like the WWF even though that is not what you said at all. There is an *association* of WWF = Panda, which affects the meaning of the statements.

NTs perceive many associations when they hear something, and make many possible inferences. They get all those resulting messages at once; they hear a sort of a fuzzy cloud of messages, not just the specific literal thing that was said.

Knowing how words get interpreted by other NTs, an NT who is speaking will say things that convey a variety of simultaneous meanings, but will craft the specific words so that the listener will get the intended message cloud. The speaker is also careful to avoid words that could be inferred to mean anything that the speaker does not want to convey.

The pattern of inferring by association is related to the pattern of multi-level communication. NTs say thing on multiple levels, and they also convey a fuzzy range of meanings when they speak.

Because of this pattern, an NT who *intends* to insult the WWF might say those words from the example ("Your logo is a panda. I don't like pandas.") Those words would only be spoken like that in order to insult the WWF.

There is a very important corollary to the idea of communicating in a fuzzy range of meanings. I have noticed in my years living with the NTs that they can miss shifts of meaning that are brought about by a single word. They might ignore the literal meaning of a sentence if the whole seems to be going in another direction, or have poor comprehension when the meaning rests on a small point.

Because NTs use many cues including nonverbal ones to comprehend something, they develop expectations, which help tell the story. If the literal meaning contradicts the expectations set forth by other cues, the literal meaning may be overlooked.

Has this happened to you?

In the play, Ivan points out in a literal but indirect way that the address 321 Broken Arrow is the address on the wedding invitation, and Carmen is meant to understand that the wedding is taking place at that address. He is leading her to make the connection between the wedding and the address of the property that she plans to demolish. Carmen instead understands that she is being invited to the wedding. She takes the indirect and self-deprecating *tone* as the message, and chooses to ignore the literal message. Once she determines that Ivan is inviting her to the wedding (which he is not), it no longer matters what he actually says; anything he says will be ignored or fit into what she expects to hear.

Pattern 26. Drawings of associations

When NTs make a visual map of some abstract concept, it can reveal their belief web in a visual form. Here is a diagram I saw recently:

The Sending and Receiving Systems

Entitlement

Eligibility

Sample diagram revealing how NTs think in associations.

You might wonder: Why are the runners going in opposite directions? Why the runners are on top of the hedges? Is one of them Sending and one Receiving? Is Entitlement the entrance and Eligibility the exit, or the other way around? Although it is tempting to try to draw various literal conclusions from the drawing by asking such questions, I concluded in this case that those literal meanings do not exist. The artist was probably not trying to convey any of those specifics.

My guess is that the purpose of the diagram is to say graphically that *the eligibility for some entitlement program is confusing, in the same way that a hedge maze is confusing.* Perhaps the artist did not know what the eligibility requirements were. Perhaps she felt that the program was changing fast. The diagram reveals the associations of the artist. I have no way of knowing what her beliefs are, but I'm guessing something like this:

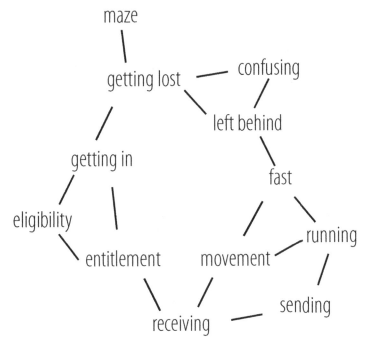

Possible belief web of the artist who created the diagram "Sending and Receiving Systems."

Another common diagram type is the "triad." When there are three of anything, people like to arrange them in a triangle and connect the corners, and often draw other things around the three corners. (You can find hundreds of such drawings by searching the internet for "triad diagram"). The connections usually just show that they are associated, not that they have any specific relation. They are not necessarily members of a superset, or mutually disjoint, or equal in value - they are just associated in the culture.

Pattern 27. Behavioral shortcuts

NTs use shortcuts in perception, cognition, feelings, and responses, and can make quicker connections because of it. The shortcuts are the use of symbols that approximate a collection of details. This shortcut is closely related to the lumping pattern, where collections of things are taken to be the same thing. This is also similar to the metaphor of the forest versus the trees: the forest as a whole is the shortcut for the trees.

Using a shortcut makes it quick to assume a general pattern based on a small amount of evidence. For example, a person looking down is often believed to be sad (even if there is actually a different reason for looking down). Other gestures and behaviors are taken simplistically as indicating some absolute conclusion.

When using the shortcut pattern, the person may be very lax about accuracy, to the point that they are making incorrect assumptions. The simplest, most obvious interpretation of a situation may not be correct. But if many people share the same interpretation, it becomes "true" in the sense of social reality, and is then believed at the group level to be absolutely correct.

Consequently the shortcut pattern is used purposefully in behavior. Using the example of "looking down = sad," an NT might look down while knowing how that behavior will be interpreted. If he wants to communicate being sad, he will look down; if he wants to hide being sad, he will intentionally avoid looking down. Therefore the purpose of the behavior can be to communicate.

The "Intentional display" pattern, below, will take this idea further.

In the play, Donna looks up to indicate piety, and Angel looks down to indicate being forlorn. Later Donna puts her hands on her hips to specify anger, and Angel rolls her eyes. These actions were done to say something, just like words are used intentionally to say something.

When behaviors are used to communicate feelings, the feelings may or may not have actually existed.

Pattern 28. Indirection

NTs like to be indirect. Indirection is seen by NTs as essential to keep the peace, be polite, and maintain relationships. It's pervasive and foundational; it is not a verbal trick that is occasionally added on to other communication. Indirection is the norm, and being direct is the exception used only when drafting legal documents or other specialized communications.

There are several kinds of indirection employed in neurotypical communication.

1. *Indirection using metaphor.* Metaphor is a kind of substitution in communication - a manner of speech using a substitute or proxy for the intended thing. A great example from the book *Look Me In the Eye* is when a taxi driver approaches an apartment complex to drop off the passenger, and asks "Where are you?," which is a substitute for "Which apartment is yours?" The autistic passenger said "I'm right here," because she missed the metaphorical indirection. In order to decode metaphor, the listener has to test multiple meanings and determine which is the suitable level of indirection for the current situation.

2. *Indirection using ambiguity.* The more ambiguity there is, the more meanings are included in one expression. For example, the sentence "I'm not going to be there until you get there" does not specify the reason for being late. It leaves open the possibility that the lateness is an invitation to go together, or a threat of some kind. A statement that has a tone/inflection or gesture that doesn't match creates an ambiguous way of saying it. A message given as a question or with a "maybe" (or some other noncommittal word) or in the subjunctive mood can express vagueness, or a range of possibilities without nailing down one of them. An autistic listener might be confused, and not seek out multiple meanings, or might assume the simplest one. (In the example above, the autistic might understand that the speaker has a prior commitment until the approximate hour when she happens to be going, and nothing more than that). In order to decode ambiguity, the listener has to understand all meanings at the same time, without discarding some of them or settling on any one.

Sarcasm is the particular case of ambiguity that includes two opposites in the same expression.

3. *Indirection using subtlety.* Subtlety dwarfs communication. Gestures can often be more subtle than words, although grand gestures can also be more blatant than words. Voice inflection can be subtle or blatant. In order to decode subtlety, the listener has to have enough sensory integration to be able to process all the senses at once.

4. *Indirection using abstraction.* The more abstraction there is in an expression, the more separation it has from precisely defined words and actions, and the more particular it is to one culture. Free-floating symbols are the most abstract symbols. In order to decode abstract (cultural) meanings, the listener has to have memorized the mental map of the language and culture (including postures, variances in speech, and other culturally prescribed behavior).

Examples of different kinds of indirection:

Here's an example of statements about afternoon drinks:

- "I want tea." This has no type of indirection.

- "I want either coffee or tea." This is ambiguous, but otherwise direct.

- "It's three o'clock, sir." This is cultural, but unambiguous. (There is no mistaking the intent, as long as you know what normally happens at 3 in this household.)

- "Isn't it time for a stroll or something?" This is ambiguous and cultural.

- "Ahem" (making sound of dry throat) This is subtle, but unambiguous and otherwise direct.

- "What's on?" or "What's for tea?" This is metaphor (on = the kettle on the stove; tea = time for tea and/or other drinks or food)

This example is meant to make clear how each kind of indirection is separate. It is not the case that verbal speech is always clear and non-verbal is subtle or ambiguous; it can also be the other way around.

Why is indirection used? I can attempt to answer this first by saying that NTs communicate how they think, and they think in associative ways. That is, their minds are a web of concepts and words and other cultural notions, that all relate to each other. In order to convey the whole chunk of the web to another person, it can't be broken up; one piece of it in isolation is an inadequate way of presenting something, because things derive their meanings from all the other things that they are associated with in the web. Consequently, communication has to be soft, repetitive and multi-faceted. They are always "getting at" something instead of isolating the single thing to say.

The corollary to this is that the history of a relationship can be re-written. If something was subtle, you can say it didn't happen. If it was ambiguous, you can change the "real" meaning after the fact. If it is culturally abstract, it lacks precision in meaning in the first place. The more re-writing that can be done, the greater sense of consistency. Inconsistency causes cognitive dissonance.

NTs will say indirectness is part of being polite and non-aggressive. If the alternative directness is negative, such as a judgment of bad character or hate, then indirectness still communicates but lets the other person down gently. Instead of being fired, you might be "let go," creating the image of a bird being set free. It's a social story that props up or invests social currency in the person who is actually being fired. It prevents the person from "losing face" - that is, keeping integrity or keeping the the identity intact.

If something is indirect, in can also require extra attention. If it is outright enigmatic, it can require study to figure it out. The more work one does to receive a message, the more one has invested and therefore the more meaning it might carry.

Indirection can cause problems for autistics. If we cannot or will not operate in their indirect way, our directness clashes with the norm. Isolating a single direct point (perhaps more common to autistics) can feel harsh or blunt to them, even rude or threatening. Their need for indirection is shared by the vast majority of the population, and provides a great deal of security. There is no point to them in risking the aggression, impoliteness, and rigidity that is caused by a more direct way of speaking.

Consequently some NT-to-autistic attempts to communicate can be stymied by both parties refusing to or unable to adopt the other party's stye. The NT might say "Why should I have to resort to direct language? That would be rude! Normal people can understand me, so he ought to be able to as well. If I'm that rude, I risk retaliation, or a loss of my reputation." On the other hand the autistic might say

"Why can't he say precisely what he means? He never gets to the point. I shouldn't have to wait through all this banter."

Recap

The communication patterns of NTs explain how they share their internal belief webs with each other. Communication occurs on many levels, of which transferring information is only a small part. The nonverbal message is the more important part, and words are stretched out and repeated in order to give time for the nonverbal message to get across.

Small talk is used to test the other person's identity and while being able to back out of anything that was said. Behaviors are used to communicate rather than just to accomplish things.

NTs do not process complex rules in their communication; they mainly just process pre-built associations.

There are various kinds of indirection in NT communications (metaphor, ambiguity, subtlety, and abstraction), which allow them to express many things at once and keep the past open to shifting interpretations in the future.

Patterns of Feelings and Display

The patterns in this chapter relate to the NT process of deciding and displaying "who I am," morals, and the relational emotions.

Before getting to that, the primary, **internal emotions** should be mentioned first as background. Internal emotions are those that humans generally share with other mammals, which set the basic faculties into action to meet the animal's survival needs. Internal emotions include fear, anger, contentment, sexual desire, and love. These drive the faculties of killing, hiding, planning ahead, and family/tribal connection - which ultimately allow people to survive.

By contrast, the **relational emotions,** like pride and offense, are more complex than the internal ones, and are shaped by the culture rather than just by nature. These terms - internal and relational - were developed for this book.

This chapter also includes **defense mechanisms**, such as repression and projection, which are techniques for maintaining an identity when reality conflicts with the internal symbolic map.

In the next scene of the play, the basic NT patterns of identity and display are stressed by the characters' interactions.

Scene 6 of The Lockstep Tragedy

In Star's bedroom. Angel, Valerie, and Donna are helping with make-up and the wedding dress.

STAR: Val, you're the best.

VALERIE: Yes I'm the best, but if you *look* as good as me, you're the best too. Isn't this fun?

STAR: I'm just scared.

VALERIE: When you're all dressed up, there is nothing to be afraid of.

STAR: I can't wear this and be elegant like you.

VALERIE: You can do anything you set your mind to.

STAR: Thanks. But why did you abandon me yesterday?

VALERIE: Well, after James left, he kind of didn't really go, so we kind of hung out. Just don't tell, Starling, OK? I think he might be the one!

STAR: OK.

DONNA: Angel, go get those things for her sash.

ANGEL: I'd help, but she doesn't love me any more and I'm writing a poem anyway.

DONNA: Angel, you're fifteen. Act like it. [*to Star, handing her a tiara*] Here, you need to try this on.

STAR: So what's with Carmen? She wants to convert everyone and she never shuts up.

DONNA: That's not nice. We have to be nice to her anyway. Try it higher up.

STAR: She can't actually take the house away from us, can she? I mean, it's yours, right?

VALERIE: That was for real?

ANGEL: They pay rent, Star. That means it's not really ours. Don't you know anything?

DONNA: Girls, hush. It's going to be OK. Tony takes care of that. Now Angel, I think you need to apologize.

ANGEL: Sorry, Star. I thought you knew that.

STAR: [*smiles*] It's OK.

DONNA: I still don't think the tiara is right. How do you want me to put this on you, or do you want to go without it? We can do that too.

STAR: How am I supposed to know?

ANGEL: [*taking the tiara, teasing*] Do something with this! Make up your mind! You can't spend all day on the tiara. How about like this? [*puts it on Star's head backwards and laughs*]

STAR: Go away, you girl, you are smothering me.

DONNA: Get off her; you aren't helping. [*removes the tiara and places it in a drawer*] There, I've fixed it.

STAR: I guess I should have told you about that guy who came yesterday.

VALERIE: You believed that... James would...? [*returns to daydreaming about James*]

DONNA: [*suddenly concerned*] Who are you talking about?

STAR: [*nervous*] Well, someone came yesterday. He said he was demolishing the house, this house. He called it a "demo" like it was no big deal.

DONNA: Tony was supposed to hold this off! He was supposed to be the man. Now I have to come to the rescue. But don't worry about it for today, Star honey.

STAR: [*agitated*] He said it would *be* today!

ANGEL: I hope they knock it down during the wedding. We haven't suffered enough yet.

Donna slumps onto the bed.

VALERIE: Hold on, Ivan's dad's girlfriend owns this house?

DONNA: No she doesn't! Oh, I don't even know who owns it. I guess she does.

VALERIE: That could get ugly. But it will be fun to see her crash and burn.

STAR: Where are you going to live? [*fearful*]

DONNA: Your dad *is* going to work this out. That's his way of showing that he loves us.

VALERIE: Star, it's time! [*time for the ceremony*]

Pattern 29. Identity from group

NTs often define themselves as members of a group. For example: I'm an American, I'm a girl, I'm a receptionist, I'm a goth, etc.

They don't merely *indicate* membership in groups; *the membership is in itself part of the identity.* They might define themselves *primarily* as members of groups, and any other kind of identity is secondary.

Group membership appears to be more fundamental to some NTs than obtaining food and shelter. (This assertion is based on how seriously they take threats to their identity group, as explained in the next chapter.) People are all different of course, but to varying degrees, NTs are conscious of, and protective of their identity groups.

Group identity shapes values and beliefs. NTs may say that they have their own independently chosen set of values, and that they join groups that share those values. But the opposite is also a prevalent pattern: NTs get accepted into a group, and then adopt the values of that group.

The political identity of Americans is an example that makes this point easy to grasp: An NT who "is Republican" comes to believe things like: that killing unborn babies is abhorrent, medical care should be based on the ability to pay, and that double taxation suppresses businesses. An NT who "is Democrat" comes to believe the opposites: killing unborn babies is acceptable (except they would use different terms because those words make it sound like something they don't believe), medical care should be based only on medical need, and that businesses should pay more tax because they have money. Regardless of any rational connection between these ideas, people polarize themselves based on their chosen identity group. Someone's opinion about abortion essentially controls their opinion about taxes and vice versa. It can even happen that when one side thinks of a solution to a problem, those on the other side will adopt the view that a completely different solution is necessary, even if they never promoted their solution beforehand. They just need to maintain opposition because their identity as members of the opposing group demands it.

I find I can easily be confused about the level of independence that NTs have, and to what extent group memberships control their whole identity. Most people are not harshly indoctrinated into the passive acceptance of a belief system, and they arrive at their beliefs and personality through their unique life experiences and free will. Therefore they might deny any connection between their identity and group membership. But the question of indoctrination is not really what this pattern is about. The groups that they derive identity from include those groups that they have freely joined or associated with. There's a confusing duality: An NT feels he is a unique individual, but at the same time, he freely chooses to join with other unique individuals to form groups around which they freely coalesce their identities.

Pattern 30. Intentional display

Intentional display is the intentional showing of a feeling that is chosen by words, expressions or gestures.

Display in NT adults is very different than children. Children run and jump and use other movements that show emotions, but are not consciously deciding to display a particular emotion. Through practice, adults get rid of the free movements and exclamations, replacing them with words, gestures and other controlled movements that tell the story that they want told. NT adults can appear very artificial to children and autistics because so much of their affect is controlled by choice.

NTs often lump together the internal state of something and the display of something. For example, "he displays an understanding of fractions" is equivalent to "he understands fractions" from those speakers who don't distinguish display from the internal state.

The chosen feeling to display is not always what is *really* felt; the inner world may be repressed, as explained by some of the patterns later on. The purposes of choosing an emotion to display include association with a group, exporting a belief, manipulation, and vying for rank. It also changes the actual feeling to display the feeling. You might hear advice like "Just act like someone who is having fun, and you will eventually start to have fun." So in that sense, intentional display is not always a lie; it is a way to make something true.

Intentional display is one of the main patterns that distinguishes adults from children at a glance. NT adults control their emotions most of the time and are not swept up in an apparently uncontrollable surge of emotions. They learn this by practicing intentional display, which brings their actual emotions in line with "appropriate" (culturally prescribed) emotions. Adults will even tell children "don't be sad" or other direct commands of what their emotions should be.

Here is a table summarizing adults and children side by side in general terms. The last row contains some examples.

Children (and autistics) are limited to:	Adult NTs also learn:
The "because of" model of behavior (behavior is controlled by feelings)	The "in order to" model of behavior (behavior is used to convey feelings)
feeling → behavior	desired state → behavior
tired → lie down energetic → run happy → smile	relaxed → lie down attractive → run happy → smile

This arrow (→) should be read as "causes": For children, feelings cause behavior; for adults, a desired state can also cause behavior.

Notice that "happy → smile" appears on both sides. On the children's side, being happy involuntarily causes a smile; on the adult side, the desire to be happy, or at least to appear to be happy, leads to a voluntary smile.

The example of "attractive → run" is shorthand for: I want to be attractive, so I will run (for fitness, perhaps in a visible location, in order to be seen).

I also want to talk about running in some more detail. Suppose you exit from a store, and run across a parking lot to your car. You may be running because you need some exercise, or you are happy, or you want to see how far you can jump, or for some other reason. But NTs generally don't do this (even if there is a good reason to) because someone might believe they are running because they have stolen something or are running to attack someone. The common belief is that "running = guilty." They don't want to communicate bad intentions, so they don't run, whether or not they actually have bad intentions. This and thousands of other behavioral shortcuts are acted out all day long, in order to communicate "I have not stolen anything, I'm not attacking anyone" etc. Through their intentional actions, they "say" things that control what others believe about them.

In the play, Carmen is apparently delighted by the idea of townhouses. But is she actually *happy* the way a child is happy to see a puppy? I would say she is only *displaying* delight, and displaying it on purpose in order to further other people's interest in it, be high ranking in the group defined by that associated collection of beliefs, and make money from it.

Everything Valerie says is a calculated display, to create a relationship, obtain a favor, or make herself appear favorably. She has no inner world under her displays; she has become her display. This does not mean she is faking happiness while hiding a tormented dark side; in fact she is quite unified and effective living in the display world. It is not a lie; there is no distinction between her display and her truth.

Social communication is so fundamental to the life of many NTs that they literally do everything as an act of communication. They dress, walk, eat and carry things as a portrayal of their identity. Each tiny action from reaching for a door handle to placing a jacket over a chair is done with the thought of how the action will appear to others. And they assume that every tiny action done by others is done for the same reason.

Big actions are also done to convey messages. For example, in 2010 there was a national debate about the plan to build a mosque near the former site of the World Trade Center in New York. The debate centers on the "messages" sent by the action. For example, one view is that the message means that Islam is victorious over Christianity. Another view is that the message means that the US is a nation of inclusion and openness. Or that the Muslims want to build it there as a message of threat. Or that we don't care about the families of the victims of the 9/11 attack. The building will act as an intentional display of messages.

Pattern 31. Personality construction

NTs choose their displayed feelings and traits, and based on this, construct their whole personality. Primarily from about age 12 to 17 (adolescence), they try on different ways of being, like trying on shirts. The "shirts" they are trying on are identity groups, their role in the groups, and how they display themselves in that role. When they develop a display that works for them, they spend the rest of their life armoring it, to make it impossible to deconstruct. NTs can be very fearful of deconstructing all that hard work.

The constructed "self" of the adult is a cultural symbol to all others who know him.

In the play, Angel, who is 15, is trying on the idea of relentless suffering, and practicing saying "no one loves me," but those ideas don't arise from her actual life circumstances. It's a trial personality. Those around her probably feel she is going through a phase and do not actually believe she is suffering.

The older characters have more developed permanent personalities that serve to protect and sustain their weaknesses. For example, Star does not engage and always wants to be left alone. Her story is "I can't." Although not developed much in the play, she might build her personality to show herself as a wise observer, who is above interpersonal problems, and values independence. Those displays of personality allow her to avoid ever facing her fear of engagement; therefore the personality locks in the weakness.

By contrast her father Antonio (Tony) is also independent but in a different way - a can-do way. He avoids his own need for growth by creating the story of always being right. He has built up a personality of being a jokester, and an efficient, decisive commander. Those personality traits protect him from ever having to face choices in his development.

Pattern 32. Delusional self-awareness

Some NTs are more self aware than others. In the pattern of delusional self-awareness, the person is certain about their internal state, and attempts to display the chosen state, but this is far from what actually is happening emotionally within them.

In the play, Paul is always representing himself as being the most calm and reasonable person around, but is terrified in a way that he can't access: anything unexpected is a threat. He might say that nothing is threatening, but that is the delusion. Donna believes she is helpful with the tiara, and even "offers" to allow Star to *not* wear it. The delusion is that Donna believes she has a role in that outcome: she helped Star decide not to wear it, making her appear important.

Pattern 33. Value judgments

A value judgment is an opinion on the worth or rightness of something, and more specifically, an attempt to change the truth value of something. In terms of the liquid truth pattern, making a value judgment is an attempt by force of words to affect the level of truth, or the associations to a symbol in the shared belief web. It is *not* a reflection of personal experience. For example, "I got sick because I ate at McDonald's" is a judgment of ones own experience (which may or may not be accurate), but "McDonald's is a horrible place" is a judgment of value.

Value judgments can be made in several flavors:

- Direct - For example, "Hummers are awesome."

- Identification of what other people "need" - For example, "That guy needs to be locked up." (meaning: he is bad, or I need to be protected from him) or "You need to get your work done." (meaning, the work is good, or the punishment from me will be worse)

- Identification of what other people want - For example, "You want to graduate with honors."

- Expectations - For example "You are going to mess up my books." Or, "I just know you will make Mommy proud."

NTs often receive a value judgment as a cue to conform their belief web to the judgment. The listener will adjust and say to herself: I like Hummers too, I want to graduate with honors, I will make Mommy proud, etc. Such judgments are used extensively when raising children to produce a copy of the parent's mental map in the child. However, if the child later joins a different identity group, the judgments won't necessarily work across group lines.

Examples from the play include Angel not being mature enough for her age, Carmen wanting to "convert everyone," and Valerie telling Star, "you want it to be romantic."

The number of value judgments you might hear varies a lot by subculture, and by the person. Have you ever felt oppressed or alienated by too many judgments, or didn't know how to answer them? The speaker is usually not using them as an attack, but is more likely trying to make a conforming-type connection. If two people conform to the same beliefs, that forms a connection. If you are autistic and cannot conform in that manner, the connection attempt could fail.

Pattern 34. Make-feel

Recall from the pattern of influential communication (page 78) that a big purpose of communication is to bring about a desired emotional state in others. In the pattern of make-feel, one person makes another feel happy, or makes her feel sad, or any other emotion. NTs can hurt (and repair) each other's feelings. Also recall from the pattern of lumping (page 49) that "things are what they appear to be," so saying "I'm sorry" is functionally the same as feeling sorrow, and by force of words, causes the repair of the other person's emotional state.

An example of making someone feel something in the play is when Valerie calls Angel "Angel-cakes": this puts Angel in the same group as Valerie, which is an improvement in status because Valerie is dominant. Another example is when Donna says "What I have to put up with!" and a third example is when Angel insults Star ("Don't you know anything?") and then apologizes and repairs the hurt feelings.

A group of NTs gives each other control and responsibility for their inner states. For example, if A makes B mad, then it is A's responsibility to fix B's anger. People in the helping professions will often say that we all need to take responsibility for ourselves and not blame our feelings on others, but in actual practice, the responsibility is shared. Many American parents shame their children for hurting another child's feelings, and instruct them to "say you're sorry," which indicates the belief that the child has control over the other child's feelings.

Scene 7 of The Lockstep Tragedy

Still at the house, a reception after the ceremony. Paul and Tony talk over drinks.

Paul: Quite a ceremony. You'll get to do this twice, Tony.

Tony: It's an honor. I expect your son will live up to our expectations, although I'd say he is a little financially irresponsible, wouldn't you agree?

Paul: I don't know where he could have learned that from. [*trying to be funny*]

Valerie enters, followed by Angel.

Angel: Who wants to hear my poem? I spent all day on it. It goes - "sharp, piercing wedding bells, poisonous white cake, another day..."

Valerie: Angel hush! No one wants to hear you. Don't you have any common sense?

Paul: [*to Valerie*] I'm sure that's not appropriate at this time.

Angel: [*to Valerie*] When's the right time, Miss President? When my bookcase falls on me and I'm pinned there gasping my last breath, then is *that* the right time? You all are being so dramatic.

Paul: A wedding reception is supposed to be a celebration. Come on, let's stick with the program.

Donna enters.

Tony: [*to Valerie*] Tell the bride to get out here.

Valerie exits, followed by Angel, leaving Paul, Tony, and Donna.

Donna: Tony, she's coming. She's just - fixing her hair. Ah, what a day! She was so lovely. Do you remember our wedding? Everyone had such a good time.

Tony: Oh yeah. That's when you learned not to run away. [*makes a fist*]

Donna: Well I'm not running from anything. We'll be together a long time, right here.

Tony: Some people might not want us to stay here a long time, but *some people* can talk to my face if they have a problem with me.

Paul: I suppose they should. If you would just be a little nicer about it, I'm sure everything will be all right.

Tony: Who should? You have a problem with me? [*pretend boxes Paul*]

Paul: Still got it in you, huh?

Donna: He's our comedian, sure enough.

Tony: I'm hungry. Donna, go get me more of those bacon things. [*Donna goes*] "Comedian" - damn it. Don't get married again, my man. Some days I wish I didn't have someone calling me a damn comedian.

Paul: Carmen doesn't want to get married anyway. She's, uh.. [*falters*]

Tony: A tramp? a bitch? What is she, Paul, and *why* are you with her?

Paul: That's not nice! [*firmly*] She's actually really interesting, and not like anyone else I've ever dated.

Tony: Interesting? You need to get out more, buddy. - Sorry, but someone has to tell you. That's what friends are for, right?

Donna returns with food.

Donna: Here, dear. I should go talk with the Binghams.

Tony: Go then.

Donna: [*explosively, but quietly to Tony*] Just go? Is that how it is? You didn't lift a finger for this wedding and you're not even talking to the guests! You get what you want. It's *never* going to be my turn. [*exits*]

Action follows Donna as she meets Star and Ivan, entering, followed by Angel.

Star: [*to Angel*] Can you just *look* like you're having fun, for me, for today?

Angel: Just try and make me.

Ivan: [*to Star, noticing Tony is agitated*] Sounds like the typical family crap. What's up with ol' Tony-O, did the Yankees win or something?

Star: I don't even care any more. I'm moving out, and we're gonna be self-sufficient. [*to Donna, brightly*] I'm so glad everyone came.

Donna: Oh, you were wonderful!

Pattern 35. Confidence

Confidence indicates the level of force with which cultural propositions are sent out by one person and received by another. It is important to understand that in social interaction, confidence is not necessarily related to its scientific meaning of the probability of accuracy. A person can be extremely confident about something that is not true at all in any literal sense.

Confidence is to communication as certainty is to knowledge. The pattern of certainty has to do with how strongly a belief is held in the mind; the pattern of confidence has to do with how effectively a belief is sent out to others.

People attain power over others through their mastery of confidence. The more confidently something is said, the more it is believed, and the more the person becomes an authority. It is only possible to rise to power politically if one has a high confidence level in everything he or she does, and expresses that powerfully so that others are practically forced to believe.

Pattern 36. Common sense

When exhibiting "common sense," NTs are preoccupied with what is *appropriate* (conforming to culture), instead of what is true or beneficial. If there is some choice to be made, the work of deciding what to do consists of reflecting on their shared beliefs and determining which option is the least disruptive to those beliefs. (Common = shared; Common sense = shared web of beliefs.) When "common sense" is used as a justification for an action, this is a bit like saying "because everyone else does it." When common sense is put into effect, the action manipulates the environment to more closely match the shared belief web of the doers.

Consider the example of the choice to use gasoline or lighter fluid to start a wood fire. Without any prior knowledge of the subject, a person might not know that gasoline is more more flammable than lighter fluid, and might not have enough experience to know what the dangers are, or what other questions to ask. Using common sense in this situation would mean *not* thinking about it, but instead just doing what other people do in the situation ("Lighter fluid is appropriate, so I'll use lighter fluid."). The alternative approach would be to experiment, ask questions, and understand, then apply knowledge of the subject to get the best results. In this example, common sense is probably safer than experimentation, since experimenting with gasoline can be dangerous.

Another example of common sense is the decisions by government to spend money to achieve some sort of outcome, like dealing with traffic congestion. Often these expenses are justified by studies that ultimately only reflect a shared sense of what is *appropriate* and are not based on an analysis of the *actual effects* of the project. There may be a problem (traffic congestion) and a proposed solution (an urban rail system), and when the project is all done, there is the same amount of congestion as before. When that kind of thing happens, the "solution" was likely based on common sense rather than on an analysis of actual effects. In this case, applying common sense resulted in an undesirable outcome or zero improvement.

In the play, Angel begins reading a poem that sounds like it might be very negative, and Valerie stops her, saying "Don't you have any common sense?" Common sense in this situation indicates the shared collection of beliefs around what is appropriate at weddings. Paul also acts as a self-appointed monitor of what's appropriate and tells people - for example, "I'm sure that's not appropriate at this time."

111

Common sense is a pattern that inhibits change, and protects people from mistakes. But when common sense is the only pattern affecting decisions, then large, complicated problems cannot be solved.

It's hard for NTs to talk about common sense to others who aren't NT; so it is hard for visitors to understand specifically why they do things when the reason given is "common sense." They might say "It's just obvious!" This is because the shared belief web is so inherent to the way they think and perceive, that they can't easily separate it out. If you have been blamed for not having common sense, you may be at a loss as to where to find this elusive thing. You can't just develop common sense; it is an adult effect of having grown up consistently using the fundamental patterns like symbolic filtering and sensory integration.

Pattern 37. Groupfeel

Groupfeel is the phenomenon of a group making the assumption that they have the same views and feelings. For example, when a person feels sad watching a movie, she might say "You felt so sad at the end." Using the pronoun "you" (unstressed) indicates the assumption that the other person, or all people, feel the same thing as she did. Since NTs are adaptable and always running on partial information that is in a state of change, it is not really possible for them to *actually* have the same views. So the phenomenon of groupfeel is mainly about the *assumption* of similarity.

Groupfeel is similar to the concept of "theory of mind," which is the ability to project ones mental state onto others and guess their actions and motives. Theory of mind is a concept in autism research, used to show that autistics are less capable or willing to assume that other's views and feelings are the same as ones own, or that they would act the same given the same information.

NTs have a reasonable basis for groupfeel, since their manner of thought and communication is based on conforming to the same beliefs. That is to say, when they assume a similar mental state in someone else, they are likely to be right.

Notice that the pattern of groupfeel is related to confidence: both are based on an assumption of certainty and uniformity rather than of variation.

One example of groupfeel in the play is Donna saying "Everyone had such a good time" at her own wedding. It is impossible for her to know that for sure, but if the assumption is unchallenged, then it stands as social reality.

Pattern 38. Repression

The pattern of repression is one of the *defense mechanisms* formulated by Sigmund Freud. Some of the other ones are listed as the next few patterns.

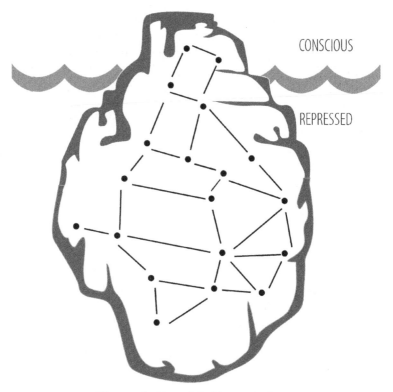

*The symbolic web is like an iceberg,
which is mostly repressed.*

All the defense mechanisms exist to keep ourselves unaware of ourselves, specifically to maintain ones constructed identity and the truth value of the belief web, and defend those beliefs against the intrusion of reality as revealed by the senses.

The web of associations is partly conscious and mostly unconscious according to Freud, like an iceberg that floats mostly under water, depicted in the drawing above.

Symbols that are **repressed** are below the surface and cannot be accessed consciously, although they still control emotions and behavior unconsciously. In childhood, repression starts with a painful memory or guilt; that item is taken away from the consciousness to protect the conscious identity, and that original symbol pulls down other symbols that are associated with it. Think of the associations as chains that pull down symbols into the unconscious level. The unconscious mind is gradually filled in that manner.

Freudian therapy using word associations causes patients to cross the line into the unconscious by finding conscious symbols that have an association with unconscious symbols. By pulling chains of symbols back up into the conscious mind, it is possible to reverse repression and, sometimes, to access the original event. Some people who have experienced violent crimes say they have "forgotten," but really they remember it very well, in a place that is sealed off from consciousness.

The patten is not limited to people with mental illness; it is probably universal. And it is not just about painful memories. Another way to approach this is: The mind cannot consider itself for the same reason you cannot see the outside of the shell that you are in; you cannot see your retina even though the retina is doing all the seeing.

Pattern 39. Projection

Projection is the defense mechanism of using qualities of yourself to describe others. If I'm boring, or afraid that I might be boring, I might accuse you of being boring. It is defensive because it allows a person to believe that he *isn't* the thing he attributes to the other.

My field observations have led me to the informal conclusion that a vast majority of what NTs say about others is projection. It is particularly clear when a person often describes many different people in similar ways. For example, when someone often accuses people of stealing, he is probably someone who steals himself. When someone often comments on how polite others are, she is probably polite herself.

In the play, there are many examples of projection: Angel accuses other people of being "dramatic" when it is clear to the outside observer that she is the one being dramatic. Tony accuses Ivan of being financially irresponsible, which Tony cannot accept is his own flaw.

Descriptions of others reveal the kind of strengths and weaknesses that a person has, even if they are not projections. Paul could have said Carmen was exciting or loving or loyal, or any number of other things, but he said she was "interesting." That reveals that Paul is concerned about where he himself is on the scale of boring to interesting. He would be less likely to comment on things about people having to do with factors that he has no self-concern about.

NTs can confuse empathy with projection. Empathy is variously defined as understanding the feelings of others (even when different from ones own), accurately guessing the feelings of others based on context and cues, or feeling the same feelings of others. Referring back to the patterns of groupfeel and make-feel, NTs may say that they are empathizing when they may be just projecting their own feelings and assuming that the other is feeling the same.

Projection as a defense mechanism keeps ourselves unaware of ourselves, but it is also a key part of cultural communication. Refer back to the pattern on value judgments, where this example was given: "Hummers are awesome." This is semantically not far from saying "I am awesome; I like Hummers." It sets the speaker close to the thing being judged; it is projecting *and* associating.

If you are living among the NTs, I would advise you to treat any adjective as suspicious. It may have a lot more to do with the speaker's identity than anything else.

Pattern 40. Denial

Denial is the defense mechanism of stating the opposite of what you (perhaps only unconsciously) know is true, to avoid facing it.

In the play, Star states "This is not happening," which is her attempt to protect her mental plan of what is happening from the intrusion of reality. Throughout scene 7, there is a lot of tension, suggesting that many of the characters are not facing the threat that was made by Carmen through James, or are not communicating it clearly. Donna goes out of her way to say "we'll be here a long time," as if by saying that, it will make it true and make the threat of eviction just go away.

Another flavor of denial is emotional denial, which could be considered an aspect of repression. People who have repressed their anger or other "bad" feelings (because they feel it is inappropriate) may deny their true feelings, and when it comes to intentional display, their display is something else (contentment, perhaps). It can come out in a very confused way.

An autistic observer who hasn't internalized the same sense of what is appropriate and inappropriate will more likely be able to see the confusion and anger under the displayed emotion, when NTs cover their "bad" emotions. Has this happened to you?

Pattern 41. Displacement

Displacement is the defense mechanism of substituting the target of a judgment, or substituting the opposition in a conflict. The person takes out their anger (or other feeling) on the wrong person.

In the play, Tony and Donna's mistreatment of each other is possibly a displacement of the resentment they feel against Carmen. They are taking out their resentment on the wrong person.

Pattern 42. Rebellion

Rebellion is adopting a group identity that is opposed to a prior authority. More specifically, it involves the intention to defy the prior authority. A common form of rebellion is teenagers who choose a group identity that opposes their parents group identity, specifically for the purpose of defying the authority of the parents.

In the play, Angel confronts Star by saying "try and make me." This reveals that she doesn't just want to do whatever she was doing, but she wants to prove to her older sister that she *can* be different.

The natural independence of autistic people is different from NT rebellion, because autistics are less likely trying to prove to anyone that they aren't following the herd. They are failing to follow the herd because they can't follow herds, not because they are seeking attention for being "different."

Pattern 43. Desert

Desert is the socially constructed quality of being deserving of reward or punishment. (The word is related to "deserve" but I like to pronounce it like *dessert* as in sweets. I'm using this little-known word only because there is no common alternative. You can also think of it as "deservingness.")

NTs can fail to distinguish the natural from the socially constructed. (Refer to the social reality pattern on page 38.) Desert is often understood as a literal quality of the person on whom it is projected. In the statement "He deserves to be beaten up because of all the horrible things he did," the moral story is that by doing bad things, he accumulated some quality of desert within him, which makes beating him up *appropriate*. The person beating him up is using common sense: he is applying the appropriate response to someone who "deserves it."

Or, desert can be about rewards: "He deserves a raise" means he did something that accumulated desert points in a mythical balance sheet, and that giving him some more money would settle that balance.

Pattern 44. Relational emotions

The NT relational emotions can be hard to grasp because they are a combination of primary emotions and other dimensions. The other dimensions are value judgments based on the symbolic web, or defense mechanisms. I'll give my definitions of some of the relational emotions, although different sources vary quite a bit on what these emotions really are:

• **Pride** is satisfaction or contentment, combined with the belief of having more value than others. (Strangely, the Christian religion names pride as a sin, yet in popular culture it is considered an asset. "You should be proud of yourself" is commonly heard from teachers trying to push students' self esteem.)

• **Vengeance** is anger, combined with the belief of having less value than others, or having lost. It could also contain the belief that the other person has accumulated a desert of punishment.

• **Rage** is anger, combined with denial about an unwanted possibility.

• **Shame** is sadness, plus the belief in having less value than others, or having desert of punishment. To shame another person is to cause their feeling of shame.

• **Guilt** is both a relational emotion and a quality applied to others. As an emotion, it is sadness, combined with the belief that one is a bad person. It can be a generalization of a single mistake to a judgment of ourselves as a bad person overall. As a quality applied to others, it is basically the negative form of desert - being deserving of punishment.

- **Envy** is possibly fear, combined with the belief of having less value than others (or less power).

- **Offense** is disgust, plus having ones identity threatened. For example, if a person is American, they may be offended when watching someone else trample on the American flag. The flag is a symbol that is chained in the symbolic web to the identity group of Americans. A nonverbal gesture that destroys the flag is a semantic attack against the network of chained symbols, and it perceived as an attack against a person's very identity. Trampling the American flag would be done precisely *because* it is such an effective way to cause pain. Remember, words and other cultural symbols can hurt. Group identity is a fundamental need, and threats to that can cause pain.

- **Schadenfreude** is happiness about the suffering of others.

- **Respect** is fear and the belief that the other has high rank.

- **Dignity** is contentment with autonomy, or being deserving of respect. (Undignified behavior causes a loss of respect from others.)

- **Honor** is similar to respect, and may involve the belief that the other has a particular rank (such as a military honor). Honoring (showing honor) can be a more codified behavior than respecting (showing respect).

- **Anxiety** is fear of not being able to control the future, mixed with the belief that we can control it. (Anxiety is not always relational.)

- **Grief** is sadness over a loss. NTs can experience very long periods of adjusting to losses if they don't adapt their symbolic web to the change in reality.

- **Resentment** is giving a "gift" with an expectation (or having something taken), and being sad about not getting anything in return.

Autistics may not feel a lot of the relational emotions or feel them in a very different way than NTs.

Recap

The chapter on feelings and display included patterns having to do with identity, display of identity, and control of the self and others and the environment based on the belief web, relational emotions, and defense mechanisms.

NTs' identity is largely derived from group membership, which can be a vague identification with a group of people, or a literal membership in an organization. Feelings are chosen for display, attributed to others, and forced onto others. Groups of NTs can assume that their belief webs, including feelings, are shared, and make judgments of others' value and decisions based on this common sense, or shared culture.

Confidence is an asset, even if feigned.

The defense mechanisms of repression, projection, denial, and displacement serve to keep unconscious parts of the belief web buried.

Patterns of Relationships & Power

The patterns in this chapter explain how NTs get what they want from others, through such techniques as forming alliances, lying, and competing for rank and reputation. NT society is organized around these competitive techniques.

Why do NTs do all this? Briefly, I feel there are two parts to the reason.

• One aspect is that these patterns help them meet basic needs like food and shelter, and feed the drives for sex, intimacy, and comfort.

• The other aspect is that these patterns are self-reinforcing, so NTs fight for symbolic victories, like the *appearance* of high status. They can be so caught in their belief web that they become slaves to their own symbols, and indulge in these patterns even when there is no benefit to their basic needs.

These are the most advanced patterns in the book. I had discovered most of the earlier patterns by age 25 or so, but I only made sense of some of the patterns in this chapter in my 30s. Therefore you may find the explanations in this chapter to be more tentative. Remember these are patterns - generalizations. You may see the patterns in some people and not in others.

In the next scene of the play, conflict builds (first unspoken), and this situation is used to show the NT patterns of rank, lying, conflict, and winning.

Scene 8 of The Lockstep Tragedy

Later in the afternoon inside the house. Some guests have gone, with Tony, Donna, Star, Ivan, Angel, and Valerie remaining. Carmen comes to the door with James, with Donna at the door.

DONNA: Carmen! I wasn't expecting you. I'm so glad you could make it.

CARMEN: You're all still here? What is this, a trap?

VALERIE: James!! [*tuning down her obvious excitement*] I mean, did you come for me, or do you know Ivan?

JAMES: I have a demolition to do today. I got to get the truck back by eight.

DONNA: [*smiling, loudly to Carmen*] Well he can take the truck back now - we won't be needing it! Come in, come in. [*They enter*]

PAUL: You're here. This is Carmen. Carmen, have you met the family? You know Tony and Donna. This is the bride, Star. That's her sister and a friend of hers.

STAR: Hello.

PAUL: Can you visit for a while? The Whitings would be considered as *family*.

CARMEN: [*aside, to Paul*] They were supposed to be vacated last week. What do I say?

PAUL: Just don't drag me into it.

JAMES: [*announcing as if from a script*] Listen up everyone, the seven-day notice period has expired. We are not responsible for your belongings, but you might want to take valuables with you. [*no longer scripted*] I don't know why the house is not vacated. This is not normal. I can't see going through with the standard procedures. [*to Carmen*] I don't know, ma'am.

VALERIE: [*comes close*] Where are we going to go - do you have a place for me?

JAMES: [*quietly*] We can get together after this.

CARMEN: We really need to clean things out of here -

PAUL: As the father of the groom, I should really step in here and -

TONY: [*yelling*] As the father of the bride, I'm gonna wipe you off the face of this earth!

CARMEN: [*energized by the prospect of a fight*] You watch what you say to me in my house!

TONY: We are the Whitings and we've lived here for years! If you think I am going to take this lying down like a little pussy, I gotta tell you, you arrogant irresponsible bitch - get your self and that jackass the hell off my property!

CARMEN: I should have known about you, Antonio Whiting. Why don't you just stay inside so I can hear you beg for mercy! James, you can go get the bulldozer off the truck *now*. [*delighted*] I have time for some champagne first.

PAUL: This is my son's wedding, not the place for this sort of language.

TONY: Dammit Paul, are you my friend or not? Because if not, I got things to say to your boy, and they ain't pretty.

Star is crying with Ivan holding her. Donna is pacing. Angel is staring incredulously. Carmen is drinking champagne out of the bottle.

VALERIE: Star baby, you'll be OK. Come on out front.

Valerie pulls Star up, followed by Ivan, and they exit. James follows after checking that Carmen is not watching. The older set continues.

PAUL: Whoa cool it Mr T., you don't want to say anything. You might sound like a greaser kid. Are you still that greased up thug?

TONY: Your mom was a whore, so shut up.

CARMEN: [*to Paul*] You never told me your mom was a whore.

PAUL: [*to Carmen*] You're drunk already. He doesn't know what he's talking about.

TONY: Just get out.

Pattern 45. Friends and enemies

Children use the word "friends" for people they play with, people who make them laugh, and people they want to give to out of love, without an expectation of reward. I maintained this childhood definition well into my 30s, thinking that everyone who referred to anyone as a "friend" was using that word to indicate warmth and affection. For NT adults, however, the word often becomes more restricted and is also used to indicate people who are in the same identity group, those you have a strategic alliance with, will stand up for you, or who are on your side in a conflict. Friends can be defined as the opposite of enemies, and friendship does not necessarily imply any warmth.

If you spend time among NTs and have been confused by their use of the word "friend," try substituting in your mind the term "strategic ally."

One way NT's make friends is by throwing tests at them. Recall the pattern of small talk (page 79), in which small talk was defined as test to gauge how trustworthy the other person is. Friendship tests can start with small talk to reveal points of weakness, and could involve actions like revealing a small secret or lending a small object, to determine whose side the other person is on. The more tests that are passed, the more solid the alliance is.

NTs can switch from friend to enemy status quickly depending on what group membership is most beneficial. Switching from friend to enemy is called backstabbing.

If you do not pass the test to be someone's friend, then he might consider you to be his enemy. An autistic person who does not participate in strategic alliances will fail these tests, and might therefore be classified as the enemy, for NTs who strongly exhibit the pattern of friends and enemies. For them, there is no middle ground.

The friends/enemies pattern is the foundation of politics.

In the play, as the conflict builds, it is expected that everyone will take sides. Tony and Paul's "friendship" is tested when Tony demands that Paul take his side. If Paul isn't a friend, he's the enemy.

Pattern 46. Categorized, scripted relationships

In the pattern of categorized and scripted relationships, each relationship falls within one of the culturally defined relationship types (Relationship types are cultural symbols.) Some common relationship types for adults are

- colleagues
- siblings
- acquaintances
- friends
- enemies
- lovers

Within each general type, there are a number of scripts, or games - which are also cultural symbols. As an analogy, with cards you can play whist or pinochle, but there is no game called whisochle. You have to agree beforehand to play one game or the other, and not shift into an ambiguous collage of two games. So it is with categorized relationships: you must either be one thing or the other, but the rule is you can't invent your own relationship type. Some common scripts are dominant/submissive, vying for power, and standing up for each other. NTs don't necessarily pick a script and play it out forever, but at any one time it forms the frame of understanding of the relationship.

NTs communicate which game is being played while simultaneously communicating the content, or moves of the game. They use multi-level communication to send and receive both levels at the same time. The game of a relationship is more primal or fundamental than the content, so the *game* is more likely to be communicated using facial expressions and gestures, while the *content* may be communicated with words. NTs adjust their understanding of the content to fit the game. This is an extremely important point. Words are rarely understood independently; they are only understood in terms of the game being played. So first the NT has to know what kind of relationship is happening, then he can understand the communicated content from that context.

To make this more clear, here is an example: My gestures tell you what relationship this is (such as classmates), and the game that is happening in that relationship (such as flirting), and my words fill in the moves in the game (such as "I lost my pencil.") There is no *information* in the statement "I lost my pencil." It is just some words that is being used to say that I'm flirting with you. The meaning depends 100% on how it is said, and 0% on the words. The same words could also be used in a different relationship (teacher-student), with a different script (student seeking positive judgment from teacher), and therefore with a different meaning.

An autistic person talking with an NT will often generate unwitting cues of the game and moves. For example, you might say something intimate, and the NT will understand that you are playing the game where the male chats up the female for eventual sex; therefore what you said was classified as a move in that game. The NT response is a counter-move - possibly a yes or no expressed indirectly. Or, you might say how you feel about the new state governor, and it could be taken as a cue that you are playing a conflict game, if the NT was in a different political identity group. In that case anything else you say would be heard as a further move in that game. If you followed up that comment with "good luck at work," that might be taken as an sarcastic insult. Once the conflict game is established, most statements can be twisted into moves justifying the game.

Because things are what they appear (to NTs), you can't back out of a game that you started accidentally. If you are autistic and have just finished saying "I lost my pencil," and at that moment, the other person thinks you want sex, then the sexual conquest pattern is the final social truth; you are stuck with it, because it cannot be simply repealed through explanation.

Earlier in the play, James and Valerie exchanged comments with very little literal meaning and loads of indications of scripted relationships. Valerie invites him to her friend's wedding, but he is not literally expected to come; she was just saying she wants to see him more, in an ambiguous way that allows her to later claim any interpretation that suits her then.

Pattern 47. Rank

Pecking order.

Like chickens, NTs establish a pecking order, or rank, within identity groups, and those groups and subgroups vie for rank in the overall culture. Some individuals are elevated to extreme popularity and become cultural leaders - in a family, classroom, church, or the whole world. NTs take cultural cues generally from higher-ranking NTs. The choice of which person is higher ranking is itself a cultural belief, so it is difficult for NTs to make that choice independently; they absorb the belief about rank from those whom they believe to be higher ranking.

Despite the fact that this pattern appears so late in the book, rank is one of the most important concepts in understanding NT behavior.

While money (buying power) affects rank, the primary definition is not wealth. Rank is primarily *cultural power.* I will get into this more in the "ultimate pattern" below.

When an NT expresses an idea, it is rarely judged solely on it own merits. The rank of the speaker plays a large role in how the idea is judged. If the speaker is not in the immediate social circle, then his credentials and popularity determine his rank.

The top ranking characters in the play are Tony and Carmen. They are not particularly pleasant to be around, so they are not the most liked, but they are good at manipulating people around them to follow their belief systems. Valerie is higher ranking than Star in their relationship; Valerie always makes the conclusive statement of what is true or should be done. Paul, Ivan, and Angel are pretty much ignored and so they are the lowest ranking.

Pattern 48. Lying & manipulation

Lying is considered a normal and acceptable thing to do among NTs, despite what they may say about it. Since a main purpose of their communication is manipulation, communicating lies is just one of the ways of achieving that purpose.

Recall from the liquid truth pattern (page 46) the example of whether the pickup truck is "hideous" or not: the choice to believe that it is attractive or unattractive is connected to the value of the person who owns it. The concept of "lying" is framed in a similar way by NTs. Here is the logic: When words are used that are not true, but they are used for a positive effect, it is not considered lying because lying is negative, and something that is positive can't be negative.

Lying can be friendly, especially about small matters, because the truth can hurt. Words can hurt and repair NTs' feelings, so the truth is not necessarily the most appropriate thing to say.

NT's usually distinguish levels of lying. **White lies** are the small and acceptable kind, such as saying someone looks nice when you don't really feel that way. Being offensive (see the pattern on relational emotions on page 120) is considered worse than lying, so NTs will usually avoid being offensive, and lie if necessary to achieve that.

Tact is slightly different than a white lie - perhaps a lesser form of manipulation than lying. Consider the question "Do I look fat in this dress?" Some possible answers are:

- "Yes, you do." - the direct truth
- "That doesn't look so good on you." - a tactful switch from what the person looks like to what the dress looks like
- "I'm not sure you wouldn't look better in the other dress." - tactful indirection
- "No, you look fine." - a white lie

Manipulating *rank* through deceit is normal and expected behavior in the social status game. For example, untrue compliments (such as "I like that necklace") can gain favor; untrue rumors can lower someone else's rank.

In the play, Donna says she's glad to see Carmen, which is rather obviously false, but she's compelled to be appropriate instead of truthful. She also claims Star is "fixing her hair" which is likely a lie to avoid saying what she is really doing, which might be more private. A lot of the denial in the play borders on lying. (Lying differs from denial in the sense that denial protects the mind from its own unconscious and is hard to control, while lying is done intentionally to deceive others.)

Pattern 49. Reputation

Reputation is the socially constructed "thing" that a person has, roughly understood as trustworthiness, and possibly other values. As a cultural symbol, it can be damaged and repaired through the force of words. NTs can make decisions about someone based on what they believe their reputation to be, rather than based on what they directly know about the person.

Pattern 50. Conflict

The simplest meaning of conflict is one course of action preventing another desired course of action, but this is only a starting point. NT conflicts encompass much more than that. Looked at socially, conflict is one of the relationship scripts - a game that is played out between people. NTs may define themselves as permanent enemies or as some other relationship type that has a competitive script.

Once conflict is established, it becomes part of the belief web and is no longer about some specific course of action, but is about the group identity of those involved. Conflicts between religions and ethnic groups persist for centuries because they become conflicts over identity, fueled by words, and they can no longer be resolved by fixing the original cause of the conflict. Likewise, personal conflicts can persist long after the significance of the original source of the conflict has faded.

Recall that the form of the script is more primal than the content. The *content* is what they disagree about; the *form* is the structure or script of the relationship, which in this case is the fact that they disagree. So in a conflict, if it is discovered that both parties actually desire the same course of action, the conflict will not necessarily be ended at that point. If the two sides have decided that they are in conflict, that becomes the structure of their story. Again, the form is more primal than the content. One party might change their position or intentionally misunderstand the other party's position in order to remain in conflict.

Third parties to a conflict (that is, people other than those who are directly conflicting) may choose sides. They will often choose a side based on the advantage to their own rank that is conferred by that side, rather than by any abstract correctness of the side. The pattern of being neutral, hearing evidence dispassionately, and making up ones mind in the manner of a judge is rare among NTs. For example, a boy might take an attractive girl's side in a conflict, believing it could lead to a sexual reward. He will then fabricate a rationale for taking her side, in order to pretend that the act of taking sides is objectively reasoned, and not simply a matter of personal advantage.

Many times, I've fallen into the conflict pattern inadvertently. I don't show that I am a "friend" of someone; that is, I don't make a strategic alliance with them. Then, they interpret my non-alliance to be the enemy relationship category. They then interpret what relationship game I'm playing by deduction from my gestures or other nonverbal means. Since I'm not intentionally giving out any game signals, I might accidentally give out signals that tell them I'm playing the dominance game - vying for power. Consequently my opinion must be the opposite of theirs (according to NT social logic). If they have stated their opinion and I have not, my opinion can be inferred, and there is not need for them to ask. If I then state an opinion that they didn't expect, I must be lying, playing "mind games," confusing them, waiting in ambush, shielding the enemy, or doing some other aggressive move.

To put this as a more concrete example, I was once accused by a transport planner of representing the "highway lobby" after I wrote a long thesis advocating public transit. I have no hope of being paid by any lobby, so how could someone have jumped to that conclusion? Here is how I think it happened. First, I told him I didn't agree with everything he said, only some of it. I possibly accidentally gave out signals that he interpreted as vying for power (in his case, it was projection, since he seemed to be headed for political office himself). Now here is where NT social conflict logic comes in: Since he was pro-transit, and I was vying for power, I must therefore be opposed to him, and consequently I must be anti-transit. (The game is primal; the content is inferred from the game.) Since I stated I was partially pro-transit, he must have concluded that I had a hidden agenda or was lying; therefore I was being paid by a lobby that uses those kinds of tactics. He decided to publicly ruin my reputation as a preventive counter-strike, and since he was far higher ranking than me, that effectively ended my involvement in that area of advocacy.

I've had many other incidents like this, but usually less overt and they often remain mysterious for years. Has anything like this happened to you?

The important thing is that conflicts among NTs are played out on the level of symbols, and might have no basis in natural-world conflicts. In other words, they might not be natural conflicts in the sense that one course of action is prevented by another course of action.

Pattern 51. Power and threats

In general, NTs are able to control each other's feelings, with words and actions. Some level of control is considered normal. For example, they intentionally do things to "make" others feel things. Words can be used to hurt other people's feelings. Saying "I'm sorry" also has a controlling effect of repairing feelings. From this basis they may also try to accumulate as much power over others as possible. Some relationships involve power balanced in both directions, and some are strongly tilted in favor of one side.

Power consists mostly of *threats* to hurt, and only rarely is the threat carried out. Many NTs seem to live out their lives within a network of threats: between any two people lies one or more potential traps - threats that have not been carried out, but which serve to maintain control that the two people have over each other.

A common source of power is knowing personal information about someone that would be embarrassing if it became public. When power-hungry NTs obtain information like this, their first thought is "how can I use this to my advantage?" One of the ways that is advantageous is to threaten the person that you will expose them unless they provide you an unrelated favor in return. Some - perhaps most - NTs will take any such opportunity and try to squeeze the most out of it, at times keeping a person under their control for years with a constant threat that is never acted out.

Common ways to create and maintain power are: lying, entering into an agreement and then breaking it, shaming or humiliating the other, and isolating the other. Having a natural asset like a skill or sexual appeal is also a potential source of power.

Political power appears to be based on a complex network of power in individual relationships. It is not given to those with the best ideas.

In the play, Tony makes direct threats ("I'm gonna wipe you off the face of this earth.") and indirect ones ("I got things to say to your boy, and they ain't pretty.") The indirect threat might be a bluff - we don't know if Tony knows anything embarrassing about Paul or is just making it up.

Pattern 52. Identity threats

Labeling or insulting a group has the effect of insulting the person who derives their identity from the group. This comes in the form of labels of ethnic groups, gender, age, or any other distinction that can be made. A threat to the group undermines a person's identity, which can feel to them worse than being starved of food.

In the play, an ethnically related slur is used ("greaser") which aggravates Tony, who responds

"Your mom was a whore." One powerful and common way to insult someone is to insult their mother, because the identity of the person is based on group membership, and the family is a group of which the mother is often the dominant authority. A shortened form of the maternal insult is just the two words "Your mother!" which omits the actual description of any insult, but can be taken as a serious threat. ("Yo mama" is an alternative which is often said as a joke but was originally a threat.)

A note about ethnicity: Human traits are variable, and there is no natural line that distinguishes races. Using the measure of color, for example, there is no dividing line between white and black. (This is explained later on in the Phenomena section.) But people still draw lines and create groups. The purpose of creating ethnic groups is primarily to make group-based threats as a way to maintain imbalances of power.

Pattern 53. Winning

In the winning pattern, the purpose is to win, regardless of what the topic is or what the rewards are. Nearly any situation can be turned into a competitive game. The game may be pointless in every respect except that it serves as a medium for determining a winner and a loser. Even if winning is the only reward, some people will play to win.

Part of the strategy in the winning pattern is changing the game to one that can be won. For example, people often change the subject during an argument when the current subject seems to be going in the other person's favor.

An important aspect of losing for NTs is **saving face**, or losing the conflict without losing honor (see the Relational emotions pattern on page 120) or reputation (see the Reputation pattern). When an NT is cornered and realizes that losing is inevitable, the strategy may change from winning to getting out with the least damage to one's rank and reputation. An argument could begin with A telling B "I demand three of your cookies!" and end with A saying "I didn't want any of *your* cookies anyway; I have better ones at home."

Some NTs have a fairness ideology that counterbalances the winning pattern. In some situations it is considered inappropriate to win by too much of a margin, particularly if there is a need to maintain a relationship between the opponents. On the other hand, if there is a conflict script being played out, then the tactic of "hit them when they are down" is prevalent - waiting to attack until the opponent is at the most disadvantaged point. Fairness is not a universal ideal, but a social technique that can be used when it is advantageous and ignored otherwise.

Like I've mentioned before, form is more primal than content. NT's can take any content (such as: whether there are any cookies left) and place it in a win/lose form, approaching the content with concerns like: who got the most cookies (that is, who won)? and if I didn't win, then can I change the game to one that I can win (who's cookies didn't get broken?), or can I save face? (I don't eat those kind of cheap cookies.)

Pattern 54. The ultimate pattern

The "ultimate pattern" is the pattern of **achievement and failure** - the idea of competing for the best place, or striving to be better. It is a social construction composed of two basic beliefs: (1) Life is essentially about achievement or success, and we are in an eternal competition to achieve the most; and (2) achievement can be measured by other people. Different people strive for different things: more possessions, more education, more generosity, more friends, more whatever. How is this different from winning? The winning pattern deals with one-on-one interpersonal conflicts, while the ultimate pattern is more about achieving rank within an identity group.

I call it the ultimate pattern because the pattern is seen nearly everywhere and crosses nearly every subculture, which makes it difficult to imagine any alternative to it. But still, it is socially constructed, not a law of nature. Pre-industrial cultures had less of the ultimate pattern; people did not expect to change their rank as quickly through their intentional efforts to do so. Now, to be clear, it *is* a law of nature to learn and develop, so that humans can more effectively meet their needs. But the idea of being measured "objectively" against ones peers is socially constructed.

Ironically, while NTs strive to conform and be normal, they also strive to set themselves apart and be unique. These are not opposite aspirations, although they may look opposite at first. The ultimate pattern is the attempt to manipulate oneself and the culture so that the person stays within the identity group, but ends up on top. It is of no use for NTs to set themselves so far apart that they are no longer included in the group. So they strive to be only *slightly* better at whatever than others, in the way that is culturally prescribed. For example, a professor may write books that may contain a handful of new thoughts, but mainly reiterate beliefs already known to the profession, and give lots of acknowledgment to her colleagues; in turn, the colleagues repay her by giving her higher rank. In this way she rises to the top of her field. If she pointed out how all their ideas were worthless and created a superior theory of her field, she would be cast out and would not have achieved anything.

To achieve high rank, the NT must either (1) change himself so that he is better than others at something, or (2) change the game, so that whatever he happens to be good at becomes valued in his identity group. Or a combination of both. Recall from the liquid truth pattern (page 46) that the shared belief web is constantly being changed as people tug associations one way or another. They are doing this to put themselves on top. For example, new sports are pushed by the people who play them so that they achieve a status of legitimacy in athletics, no matter how ridiculous they might seem to the prior generation. The pushers do that in order to spin the culture in their favor - the game-changing version of the ultimate pattern.

Many descriptions of a person that you might see in a newspaper, in a school, business or any public setting, implicitly contain the ultimate pattern. For example: "Joshua is bright and curious, and displays mathematical talent, but he loses focus easily." This "description" is really a series of four judgments about where Joshua is in the race to the top. It's hard for some NTs to be descriptive without making judgments of achievement.

Reward and punishment are doled out intentionally and serve to keep the ultimate pattern going, particularly in schools. Recall from the desert pattern (page 119) that people can be symbolically deserving of a reward. The desert is seen as coming from the achievement. The actual reward could be nothing more than a symbol of reward with no intrinsic value. A sheet of gold star stickers may cost only 10 cents, but there is symbolic value in having a high ranking person (such as a teacher) affix one of the stars on a homework paper. That symbol bestows higher rank on the achiever. The social logic is: achievement → desert → reward → rank. In schools, examples of punishment are detention or extra busy-work.

If you have lived among the NTs for a long while, you may have taken in the ultimate pattern quite deeply, as I have. Autistic readers have likely had the experience of being told they have failed, or they are **a failure**, or they will never achieve something (or anything). Have you heard this? Have you also been told false-sounding encouragement that you will succeed? If you are autistic, you probably have almost no control over external judgments, you probably are not fighting to win, so therefore you will most likely fail at the task or game that has been presented as "the thing to do." If you can unlearn the achievement pattern, and step away from it, you can learn to see it as the social construction that it is.

Pattern 55. Confidence battling

Confidence is partly real and partly feigned. Here is a situation to show what I mean by that: When going for a job interview, it is best for the NT to be confident of her job skills on account of actually having the skills. But if she doesn't have the skills, she is expected to feign confidence anyway. The word "confidence" has to do with the presentation of being sure of yourself, regardless of how grounded that is in reality.

NT's constantly battle each other's confidence, because they can, and because the most confident person wins. If you successfully attack another person's confidence, you can gain rank.

NT life is a lot like poker in this respect, and perhaps that is how poker became popular. In poker, each player attempts to display confidence that their cards are the best hand, regardless of their actual cards. A good player can detect the difference between feigned and reasoned confidence in the other players. At a certain point in the game, you often have to either get out (cut the losses) or make a challenge. The challenge involves raising the bet to the level that shatters the others confidence, so that they get out, leaving you the winnings.

A confidence challenge in life is a lot like in poker: one of the two people has to lose.

Autistics can be misinterpreted as battling confidence, in cases when they are actually just insisting on their own independent point of view.

Pattern 56. Altruism

Altruism is giving without any condition of getting something in return. I won't attempt to solve the ongoing argument over whether altruism really exists, but will assert that a large part of what may appear altruistic among NTs is only the successful effort to *appear* altruistic and not the effort to *be* altruistic. Appearing altruistic can give someone higher rank.

In the play, Donna "gives" constantly but also reminds people that she is giving, and at one point says, "It's never my turn." She was never actually giving unconditionally, but was rather hoping for something in return.

For autistic people trying to understand NTs, it is important to see beyond what they say about being a good person - giving selflessly, being fair, helping those in need, and so on. Much of the apparatus of non-profits, religions, and other instruments of "good" is driven by NTs who are in fierce competition for rank, achievement, sex, reputation, etc. Even when and if they are "nice," helpful, generous, and pious, that does not mean they have given up on all the NT patterns. All those displayed positive qualities (recall the intentional display pattern, page 98) are used in the patterns of power and relationships. Some NTs can fight for an endangered species or the rights of the poor, and they can do it with passion, and it is done in the context of their constructed identity and against an opposing group.

Please don't make the mistake of thinking that all people who appear "good" have somehow advanced beyond the patterns in this book. They may appear "good" *because* they are good at the patterns.

Scene 9 of The Lockstep Tragedy

Star and Ivan are embracing in the front yard, attended by Valerie. James is approaching.

STAR: Our wedding was supposed to be happy. I can't handle all these people.

IVAN: It's OK. We're leaving in the morning. Let's think about the future.

VALERIE: You two need to take a walk and cool off.

IVAN: Great idea! Hey Star, let's go to the park.

STAR: OK, let's go. See ya later Val. [*they exit*]

JAMES: I'm not sure what to do in a situation like this.

VALERIE: Didn't you say you have a demolition to do?

JAMES: I'd bump into you first. You're standing in the way of the house.

VALERIE: Sounds exciting. Is that your truck? It's so big.

JAMES: You wanna see it? You can check it out.

They walk over to the truck, a flatbed truck with a bulldozer loaded on the back.

JAMES: Here, check out the, uh, it has a cool radio.

VALERIE: Here's you on the radio: [*imitating James*] James here, 10-4 good buddy, yep, I'm takin' down the neighborhood. You all must submit to my big truck! I'm...

James kisses her.

VALERIE: I'm not that kind of girl! Besides I have a boyfriend already. [*She kisses him.*]

JAMES: I'll show you the radio. [*They get in the cab.*] Are you sure you want to be in that dress? It's not too clean in here.

VALERIE: Yeah, I was the maid of honor. I can't wear this again anyway.

JAMES: Are you going to get married?

VALERIE: Aren't you going too fast with me?

JAMES: Not marry *me*, you silly. You won't see me at any wedding.

VALERIE: Well it's a nice night. Your boss is still in there, probably getting drunk. Here we are.

He holds her.

Pattern 57. Symbolic sex

The sex drive fundamentally shapes culture, and the culture also shapes sexual behavior. The pattern of symbolic sex means actual sex (or any sexual action) played out according to cultural rules. All humans share some basic sexuality, but this pattern is specifically about the symbolic dimension of it. Sex is often a symbolic act - it is communicative, powerfully controlling, and meaningful. The reason this very fundamental topic appears late in the book is because it is so bound up with so many of the other patterns, and will require referring to the other patterns to explain it.

I need to warn you that I'm including topics on sexuality for completeness, but I'm an inadequate reporter of NT behavior. As a teenager, I tried to get intimate with the natives, and my failure caused so much despair that I still feel anxiety when I read or write about the topic.

First of all, **why mate?** For the purpose of this book, I will split the reasons into two groups: the animal reasons and those reasons connected with culture and identity. The animal reasons are the same as for any other species - a drive that is linked to love and our chemistry, which makes it a need for its own sake, and which fulfills the species' need for reproduction.

The reasons on the other level are connected with culture and identity. These include reasons like wanting to improve social rank through association with the partner, wanting to buy a favor or offer a favor, revenge or desire to hurt someone else, or to make the partner happy or proud, or give them some other feeling. For some, it is a competitive quest for the highest quantity of partners. For some, it is a payment in exchange for money or housing or some other need.

In addition to all of the above, there is a more subtle and widespread cultural reason: the need to conform to ones view of normal, and to appear normal to others. This could be negatively called peer pressure, or "because everyone else is doing it." Or in more neutral terms, it is because *it is expected* to find a partner who embodies the masculine or feminine identity norms and mate with that person; by doing so, one is using common sense.

My observation of NT sexuality is that the animal and cultural reasons are both necessary for most people most of the time; they only voluntarily want sex when both conditions are met.

If you are not NT, you might not have experienced the cultural side of this like NTs do. If your display of identity doesn't fit anyone's sense of normal, you may be either ignored or targeted. If you are targeted for sex, the other person's reasons are likely not the same as yours. I'll go into this more in the last chapter in the book.

The path towards sex can begin in early childhood, or even at birth if the parents enforce gender identity and if they separate groups of children by their sex. This teaches that relationships between the sexes is to be considered special, and not suitable (or not expected) for normal friendships. Many pre-teens have boyfriends and girlfriends in name only (that it, they don't touch sexually), which is an example of *holistic learning* - simulating the appearance of an adult relationship. It is also a part of *personality construction*: Just like they try on different groups and values during adolescence, they try different partners and mold their identity around the partners. Each phase of development from preliminary boyfriends, to steady partners, to engagement and marriage is a *categorized relationship*.

NTs are among those animals that have **elaborate mating rituals**. To get from a situation in which sex is not expected to actually having sex involves a lot of exchange and negotiation.

Depending on the subculture, there can be a great deal of identity layers built up around denial of the animal side of sexuality. If asked what sex is, they may say it is a "statement of love," or something like that, which has no literal meaning but serves to pretend that sex is not instinctual. There are hundreds of euphemisms for sex (making love, or sleeping together) that avoid what might be felt as a coarse or demeaning way of speaking about it. For those subcultures, the mating ritual has to keep these identity layers intact in order to maintain the denial.

Although two people might be only inches away from each other as measured in physical space (say, at a dinner table), the mental, emotional, and symbolic distance between them might be vast. NTs **cross that distance** carefully (although sometimes quickly) to be sure they won't be hurt by intimacy. Although males may be less careful, both sexes need to learn enough about the other person to decide if they want to go the whole way. We can use the patterns in this book as a way to map out how NTs cross that distance:

• **Patterns of perception:** *Sensory integration* allows them to balance the body's responses with the senses, and pay attention to all of it (also *multi-focus*). They are generally not overwhelmed with the closeness of the other person (*desensitization*) and can remain in control. They "see" qualities of the other person as symbols with specific meanings (*symbolic filtering*), such as the clothing style or posture of the other person. Those abstract symbols tell them whether the other person wants to go further or not.

• **Patterns of belief and learning:** The *free-floating symbols* of romance and courtship are communicated through their *associations* (such as wine and roses - or other markings depending on the identity group). For example, by presenting roses, it establishes the relationship category and asks a question via association. The question associated with the roses might be "will you have sex with me?," but the latter, direct question is usually *repressed* (because discussing sex is taboo), so NTs may deny any association between the direct question and the indirect symbols.

- **Patterns of communication:** *Multi-level communication* permits them to say a lot on many levels at once. They use *small talk* to practice the form of sharing, but without the content.

- **Patterns of feelings and display:** They use words and other symbols to *make* the other person feel happy and aroused. Symbols such as gifts of flowers can be sexually stimulating. *Behavioral shortcuts* are used to clearly convey feelings, such as touching and leaning forward as a sexual "move." A high level of *confidence* is necessary to secure trust.

- **Patterns of power & relationships:** Sex is not only a basic desire, but is also used as a tool in obtaining other assets, such as *rank* and *reputation*. It is often used to buy a higher status with the partner or make the partner an ally in some other conflict. *Lying* is a common way to achieve sex, in the form of confidently stated assurances. For example, the male might declare "you will not get pregnant" and thus through the force of words, that assertion becomes socially true and therefore can seem to be actually true.

That is some explanation of how people cross the distance from a nonsexual relationship to having sex, and changing the category of their relationship to sexual.

NTs do not put their belief web aside and just rely on their animal nature; sexuality for them involves their belief web and all the patterns that have been explained in this book.

I also want to discuss **the result of sex**. One result that happens the first time is that you've "had it" (gained something) or "lost it" (lost your virginity). The "thing" that is gained or lost is a socially constructed part of the identity, that is often discussed as if it is a real thing. Sex can be seen as "proof" or evidence of love. The term "to consummate a relationship" indicates having sex, or more specifically, completing the series of steps leading up to sex, which is a symbol of changing the relationship category.

In the play, Valerie and James cross the distance towards sex quickly. I'll point out a few observations from the script: They refer to themselves continuously; they refer to concepts of power; and they make "moves" that leave the door open to getting closer at each stage. A great deal of fluid thinking went into a very short conversation. If they had not both been focused on getting closer, one of them would have said something that closed their coming together, such as "Well, I'm not interested in radios." (Although that statement would have been true, it would have closed off the relationship, so Valerie chose to take the conversation another direction.)

At the same time, they were being *appropriate* and keeping their identities as decent people intact by avoiding a direct invitation to sex, which they would consider crude.

The scene ends without acting out the sex itself, or even clearly stating that it would happen. But like a lot of literature, the reader is meant to assume that any such encounter proceeds to sex.

Pattern 58. Intimacy levels

In a romantic or sexual relationship, intimacy levels are symbols that NTs share so that they have an agreement about the status of their relationship. A simple way to verbalize them is "first base," "second base" and so on, although like any free-floating symbol, people agree more on the feelings around the symbol than on the specific definition.

There is a game in going from one level to the next: one person decides to take the risk of going to the next level, where the two options are proceeding, or ending it altogether. Staying at the same level might not be perceived as an option. Starting the intimacy levels script requires communicating the direction of interest first; that is, to make it clear that this is a pre-sexual encounter, and not some other kind of relationship (help with homework, friends, etc).

The intimacy script requires exits at each level. Therefore most actions and statements are intentionally noncommittal, often able to have multiple interpretations. That leaves both the exit and the next level open. If the person says "that's a nice shirt you have," it means the conversation should continue and not end yet, and could be used to build to the next level. But if the encounter does end, then there would have been no embarrassment in complimenting the other person's shirt, and the statement could be re-interpreted as part of some other script.

Anyone who *starts* a conversation is interested in the next level, otherwise they would not start it. If they are not interested, they make that clear; if they are interested, they remain unclear by making their comments ambiguous, noncommittal, vague, or without any meaning at all. NTs usually keep talking when they are feeling connected, although the actual words don't really matter.

It is common for a relationship to start as lustful or sexual, and add trust and other components later.

When going through the intimacy levels, NTs are looking for confidence. They need a mate for their belief web, not just for the body.

One move in that game is declaring love. There is a symbol for the the move, which is "the saying of 'I love you'." Note that the symbol is the declaration, not the actual love. One person says "I love you" and this is really a question phrased as a statement. The other person then either has to accept or reject the "I love you" with a counter-move, and that determines whether the relationship goes forward or ends. That is a very simplistic explanation, and of course there are many variations. The point is, some NTs might say "I love you" *only* when attempting to get an effect by saying it, and *never* as a way to express true feelings. The reason NTs would avoid saying honestly that they like or love someone is that it could evoke the "next level" game unintentionally. It's the same reason they don't run across a parking lot, which was an example earlier in the book. They don't run across a parking lot because they don't want to appear guilty. In general, they only say and do things because they know the effect that the appearance of those things will have. In If they want to state their true feeling, they may say "someone in your shape could probably lift that with one hand" or some kind of compliment, that is meant to be understood as "I like you."

A common aspect of the pattern of intimacy levels is building a sense of anticipation by creating a conflict. Often the male wants sex and the female says no, but "no" really means "try harder." (In some cases it actually means no or not yet. In some cases the words don't reflect what the body wants, but instead they reflect what is *appropriate*.) Without having overcome a conflict, they may feel that there was no achievement, and therefore less of a reward. When the conflict is especially great and even violent, the couple can suddenly switch to sex mode ("make up sex") and this can be especially rewarding for them.

NTs appear to be generally open to changing relationships, starting new ones, and washing away the old ones. They are socially adaptable that way. There is rarely a need for a definite "yes" unless it's a marriage proposal, so they get by on "maybe" and "no" for all other occasions. And saying "maybe" to a relationship is the arena where indirect speech is king. When a person is closed to a relationship, they tend to be somewhat more direct on all levels. For example, they would turn away, not smile, say "no" or "I'm busy." But when they are open, they tend to be more indirect. Flirting is indirection raised to an art form. The golden rule of flirting seems to be that history will be re-written: all statements need to contain the possible interpretation of pushing away, as well as the possible interpretation of drawing toward. In the event you need to escape, you feel consistent, because you can claim you have been pushing away all that time.

The pattern of intimacy levels and the ones that follow are my best understanding to date. I'm afraid some readers will interpret the patterns as denigrating generalizations of all NTs. So I want to remind you that they are patterns that show extremes, and you may see the patterns with some people more than others.

Pattern 59. The sexual tease

The tease pattern simultaneously draws focus to sexuality while drawing focus away from it. It is "yes" and "no" at the same time. This pattern is divided into two parts: the physical (manner of dressing) and verbal.

A. The physical tease. On the next page is a picture of a plain person (unclothed), and the same person with a minimal bathing suit.

First, you might ask yourself which of these photos is more attractive to you, if you experience any attraction at all to the person pictured. If you are surprised to see a person with no clothes, try pausing long enough to get over that feeling, and then consider the symbolic aspect. The purpose of the photos is not entertainment; it is to inspire you to consider a pattern of behavior.

As a background point that will be used an an analogy, consider the words "singing" and "sinking". There is a whole range of sounds between those two words - for example, "singing" can be spoken with a slight aspiration of the first G making it sound a little like a K, which might make it unclear which word was intended. But despite the continuously variable way that the mouth may form sounds, the listener generally hears either one word or the other, and refuses to hear a sound that is mid-way between the two words. Anything that is mid-way is forced into one side or the other by the listener. This is an aspect of symbolic filtering.

There is a parallel between the words and covered/uncovered body parts. The uncovered breast is a symbol (in addition to just being what it is). The breast covered by a small triangle of fabric is a different symbol. (And similarly for the other visible sex organs.) The difference in meaning caused by the three small triangles of fabric is very significant for NTs. The parts are seen as either covered or not, and any ambiguous covering would be forced into one side or the other by the viewer. An eighth-inch difference in where the edge of the fabric lies can make the difference between two opposites. This is because what they are seeing is symbols, not just skin and fabric.

NTs may argue about what specifically constitutes the covered and uncovered symbols. For example, they may discuss whether a five year old girl can show nipples. (Although they are identical to a boy's nipples, they *mean* something different.) They may argue that the bathing suit in the photo below is too revealing for some situations. Despite the range of beliefs, the tendency to think in symbolic categories is common to all NTs: in this case, the two symbols of covered and uncovered.

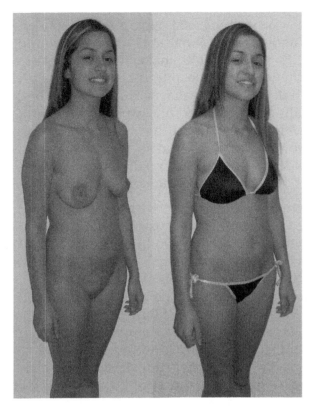

*Plain female, and the same person
with a bathing suit illustrating the tease pattern.*

In America, when covered, the person is seen to
have modesty and dignity; when uncovered, a person
is seen as indecent or shameful. It is heavily loaded
with moral value, and connected to the overall sexual
taboo. The requirement to be covered by small
triangles of fabric may even be backed by law, even
when there is no functional or health reason for it.

The physical tease pattern expresses both
opposite symbols at the same time, ambiguously.
Because she is covered, the person is "modest"
(which technically means drawing attention *away*

from oneself) but at the same time is using the bathing suit (often with bright colors) specifically to draw attention *towards* her sexual parts. Ambiguity is a type of indirection that is central to NT's verbal communications, and it can be seen the same way as central to their approach to sexuality. The bathing suit is intentionally sexually provocative as if to say "look what you can't see." Without the fabric hiding the body, the nude body is *less* sexually appealing to many NTs, rather than more.

Taboos are like denial at the level of the whole culture; taboo subjects are the organizing framework of the culture. Consequently they give rise to a lot of simultaneous opposites and doublespeak, and infuse topics closely related to the taboo with a tremendous amount of meaning.

B. The verbal tease. The other side of the tease pattern is verbal, and says "here is what you can't have." This includes flirting and playing "hard to get." Cosmopolitan magazine on-line advises women to use these tease patterns - and yes, this is advice on how to *win* the man, not on how to *lose* him.

- "Make it difficult for the man to get in touch with you, by not responding to his calls or not giving your number

- Dodge questions and avoid being direct and honest.

- Pretend to be very busy. End the phone call first, and make cryptic remarks about plans with other people.

- Talk to other men and talk about other men in order to make him jealous.

- Flirt, kiss, and dress seductively, but avoid sex for a month.

- If he passes these tests, then reward him by having sex with him."

In the end, both versions of the tease help a person achieve higher status and select a better mate by making more people want to have sex with them while retaining their sense of decency. This way they have more possibilities to choose from.

Pattern 60. Affairs

Having an affair is sex with someone else outside of a committed relationship. The common word for affairs is "cheating," indicating that one person is not staying within a set of rules. In terms of this book, the affair is when one person is not following the appropriate scripted relationship.

NTs often believe in the "true love" relationship symbol - a script in which the partners are supposed to declare fidelity (they promise not to "cheat"). They find someone to act out that script with, declare fidelity, and try to make their act true, but they might also lie about it.

I once heard an expert on this topic declare that the *only* reason people have affairs is to hurt their partner. The idea of intentionally hurting a partner was a completely new concept to me, and I could not accept that expert's view. I had always thought that sexuality was connected only to love. Love would be the incentive because love is its own reward. However, I can see now that I was woefully uninformed about NTs at that time.

A relationship is never as easy as the fairy tale version of it suggests. My current understanding is that the actual affair is usually done by NTs in order to gain power and hurt the partner. This makes more sense in the context of the other patterns of power that affairs would actually be about hurting; for some NTs, culturally defined competition and identity can be much more of a driving force of behavior than love.

Pattern 61. Forced sex

I'll start off this pattern with a personal note. I have often wondered about reenactments of forced sex on TV: how is it accomplished physically? I have never been able to visualize making my male body do what I see being done by the actors. (But it is not hard to create a mental picture of doing other crimes, so my lack of imagination is specific to this kind of crime.) I find that sex requires a lot of cooperation. In a forced situation, I would be too scared for the victim, I could not become aroused, I'd have no motivation or confidence, and I'd be at a loss mentally for techniques to subdue the victim. But in the TV reenactments, the attacker seems to have all these elements built in and ready to go instantly.

Despite feeling very remote from the subject matter, here is the understanding I've developed.

In some males, sex is closely associated with competition and violence, and it is not always closely or exclusively associated with love. Sex can be an achievement (the ultimate pattern), a measure of rank, and a symbol of allegiance; therefore it can become something to win. The symbolic (culturally learned) drive to win sex combined with the natural drive can make a person force it to occur, even if there is no love. Males can even be sexually aroused during a competitive, violent episode (extreme sensory integration, perhaps). There is an element of competition against other males, which may be arousing to them. Also, the element of hurting the victim can cause arousal.

The male seeks to gain rank over two kinds of opponents. That is, by winning in a struggle against the victim, the person gains rank relative to the victim; and by winning control of the victim, the person gains rank against other males competing for the same prize.

Some definitions: **Rape** is the crime of forcing sex (or any body penetration) without permission on a male or female victim. Some NTs classify some forced sex as non-criminal behavior, such as that between partners; while others classify it as criminal rape. **Incest** is the particular form of rape that is committed by a caretaker or someone in the family of the victim.

The victim may receive little or no physical damage, but can be greatly psychologically damaged: one incident can in some cases shatter a person's life for decades. This suggests that the damage is mostly to the mind and not to the body. On the most basic level, the person has unwanted associations between something positive (sex and love) and being attacked and terrified, and the associations darken future sexual experiences. This occurs on the level of conditioning, which is not necessarily symbolic.

I will suggest that the pain also occurs on the symbolic level, and sexual victimization causes "damage" to the belief web. For NTs, there is a huge difference in meaning between almost being killed by a car, and almost being killed in a sexual assault. In both cases, the victim is almost killed but survives - so you might reason that the effects should be equal. But they are not. In the case of sexual assault, victims report having *lost* something, which is different than surviving some other dangerous situation. The loss is part of the identity, their "virginity," their honor, dignity or some part of their completeness. They feel shame. All of these things are beliefs. The losses lower their confidence, power and rank. It is an extreme form of confidence battling. In the case of being almost killed by a car, there is no permanent loss.

A major difference is that rape is taboo (that is, widely repressed), while car accidents or homicides are not taboo. They may be terrifying and wrong, but they are not as deeply repressed. It is the taboo aspect of sexuality that both fuels the pattern of aggressive behavior and intensifies the damage to the victim. The sexual tease pattern and the forced sex pattern work together as two ways that the taboo is manifested. Incest generally involves a stronger taboo than rape by a stranger, and the identity damage to incest victims can be much worse than to other rape victims.

In summary, rape by NTs can have little or nothing to do with the desire for sexual feelings in the body, and a lot to do with causing symbolic losses and gaining rank and power.

Scene 10 of The Lockstep Tragedy

It is late at night. The house is still standing, and the guests have scattered. Paul has carried Carmen away. Valerie and James have not returned. Tony, Donna, Star, Ivan, and Angel are standing in the kitchen amidst piles of dirty dishes.

Donna: Star baby, I don't know how you'll even go on a honeymoon, much less move out, when you need me so much.

Star: I don't even need you. Besides, you're moving out too.

Donna: Tony, what about the house? That lady Carmen said she had a notice. Why didn't you tell me about this?

Tony: [*severely*] That's just a piece of paper. When you deal with me, you gotta deal to my face. We're not going anywhere. Everyone sit down and eat some more cake. [*All sit down.*]

Star: Daddy-O, … [*considers whether to ask about money for the honeymoon*]

Tony: [*abruptly*] What.

Star: It's just that … it's an injustice.

Tony: Damn straight. We will get the money together, there is no question of that.

Ivan: I felt she had a point.

Tony: What point is that, mister? Now that you have my daughter, you can tell me what to do? All of a sudden *I'm* the one who's ruining the party?

Angel: That's poetic Dad, but hardly Milton.

Donna: We're all together now. Precious, don't talk to your father like that.

ANGEL: Well, she is a rich bastard control freak ... just saying.

TONY: That's OK Donna, and she's right anyway. Ivan, tell your old man to get a life. Tell him, first of all, the Yankees suck, two, his girlfriend is an idiot, and third, he needs to find someone who isn't an idiot.

IVAN: Yes sir, that's a good point.

STAR: [*to Ivan*] My dad will go on for ages about the Yankees. But at least my family has our act together.

ANGEL: I can't believe my sister is married. We must really have our act together. I actually don't hate you guys that much.

STAR: You mean that?

ANGEL: [*soothing*] Yeah.

DONNA: The wedding really was lovely. I'm so happy for you two. I'll put together some food for the road in the morning. Some of the leftovers...

ANGEL: Those were really good cream things. There's a ton left.

TONY: And at least no one got drunk *during* the wedding!

STAR: So I didn't look like a dork? [*everyone looking at Star*]

IVAN: You looked great.

ANGEL: You did.

TONY: I was proud of you.

Donna: I can see you're tired. Are you getting an early start in the morning? [*Gets up*] I'll pack up some of the dinner too. Don't worry about anything. When you come back, we'll help you find a nice place for the baby, but you know your bedroom will always be here for you.

Tony: We are taking care of your first payment. You just come to me when you're ready, OK?

Ivan: That's very kind of you - really. [*getting up*] Anyone else want some more cake?

Donna: Stay there; I'll get it for you.

Angel: Me too, mom.

Tony: I'm going to be a proud grandfather too. A new little Whiting.

Donna: He wants a grandson, don't you dear?

Tony: It's time for a boy, but we will accept what God provides.

Donna: Maybe that's Carmen's problem [*Donna serves cake.*] She has no children. I tried to talk to her before and she just goes off.

Angel: I'd feel sorry for *her* kids. She's like running after herself with a knife and can't stop. Ivan's dad can't think for himself so he just goes along with it.

Ivan: Heh. Thank you Donna. [*eating at the table*] You know one of the nicest things about getting married is, well, besides getting married to Star, is ... I feel like I have a real mother now.

Donna: [*with tears, comes to stand behind Ivan, touching gently*] Oh dear, dear.

166

THE END OF THE PLAY

Pattern 62. Socializing

This last pattern sums up that highest achievement of NTism: **socializing.**

Most NTs participate in activities that are primarily designed for socializing (such as parties, dances, bars), and they also include socializing as part of most other things they do (work, school, sports, everything). Socializing entails being with and talking with people, but there is a lot more to it than that.

Socializing is the synchronization of the belief webs of different people. NTs share their beliefs repeatedly, and adapt to each other, changing their beliefs to conform to each other. The result is that people in the same group have the same knowledge and beliefs, use the same language, and also share the same free-floating symbols. That is, they share the same culture.

Frequently, social situations are fundamentally competitive. NTs compete for power, sex, and recognition. They love competing and conforming - and excel at it. NTs are fully functional in intense social situations; all parts work well even when there are many people interrupting and lots of things are going on at once. for example, they can think, recall information, watch people, and be present and aware in the body, all at the same time; they can even feel refreshed and invigorated after that kind of experience.

People socializing to synchronize their symbolic webs.

Unstructured non-confrontational conversations move along links in the symbolic web that is shared by the culture, and revisiting those links has several simultaneous benefits: (a) it strengthens the chains that pull liquid truth towards a true or false status, (b) it aligns the mental structure of one person with that of the other, and vice versa, (c) it makes the parties adapt to each other, (d) it makes them friends, (e) it creates culture, and (f) it can increase each party's rank in their identity group.

It takes a great deal of *time* for NTs to socialize and conform. All the time spent on conforming is an investment, that ultimately saves time in later social situations, when that knowledge is used. At the beginning of the book, I said that NTs sometimes appear to autistics as a herd of clones that waste their time talking about nothing. I hope the book convinced you otherwise: that the time spent "talking about nothing" is not wasted, but is needed for them to be able to use all the other patterns and be effective in their society.

Autistics as a rule don't socialize to conform, so we don't become experts in the culture, and therefore we can't compete effectively.

At the end of the play, the four members of the family are *doing* something when they are socializing; they are not just talking to pass time. They are mainly modifying their views to merge them into agreement with each other - synchronizing their belief webs. They share a feeling of coming together. Tony backs down from his normal commanding tone to allow Angel to make a judgment call against Paul and Carmen; the others agree verbally or silently. In the end, there are two sides as in the beginning, and the two sides are still in conflict. Everyone in the room is united on one side, supportive of each other.

It is a tragedy because nothing is resolved. The lockstep pattern prevents anyone from breaking out of the ranks of their identity group. Creative solutions to the problem of losing the house are never addressed, and even the problem itself is not directly confronted. Doing so would break the belief web.

Recap

The patterns of power and relationships were presented. The purposes of a lot of NT behavior is to gain rank, reputation, and power by creating and winning conflicts. "Friends" are sometimes defined as people on your side of a conflict, or the opposite of enemies. Each relationship belongs to one of the culturally defined types, and follows a script based on what is appropriate for that relationship type.

Appropriate or common techniques to win include lying, keeping threats active over a long time, and confidence battles. Threats against the identity group are taken as threats against a person. (Although these techniques are commonly considered to be morally wrong, they are still common.)

The ultimate pattern is the pattern of achievement - the competition for best place, as measured by others.

Intimate relationships were covered, including the symbolic path to sexual intimacy, and the tease.

The final pattern shown was socializing, in which NTs learn their culture by rehearsing and synchronizing their belief webs.

Phenomena

This chapter explains how the NT patterns are manifested in some major phenomena of modern American culture.

The patterns are meant to explain behavior in a general way, while these phenomena show how the collection of patterns play out in specific cases. The phenomena are in no particular order.

Ethnic labels

Ethnic labels include "Black," "Latino," "Chinese" and many others. The labels mean a variety of traits, judgments, and other associations, not just what the word means literally (if it has a literal meaning at all).

Consider that in literal language, a person could be a Hispanic African American White Jew, all at the same time, naming their language, origin, country of residence, skin color, and religion respectively. (The labels are capitalized, reflecting the practice of distinguishing ethnic labels from regular descriptive words.) In the symbolic web of the dominant culture, however, all those symbols are distinct and considered separate groups. The word "Hispanic" denotes ethnicity (not language). The word "White" also denote ethnicity (not color). All of those labels denote ethnicity - a myriad of associations including accent, hair styles, and music. A "Black" person could be lighter colored than a "White" person because the labels don't really refer to color; they refer to ethnicity. The symbols are free-floating in the sense that they cannot be precisely defined.

An example: A toddler may make a friend at pre-school, and the mother who self-identifies as White may say "my child doesn't even know her friend is Black." Of course this mother is not assuming the child has a problem with her eyesight and cannot see the color of her friend. The ethnic identity of the friend may stand out as highly significant to the mother, but not to the daughter. While the toddler can easily see color, it takes time to learn the significance, and to put other people into ethnic categories based on their appearance.

Subculture & Counterculture

Given nearly any cultural generalization, one can locate a counterculture or movement of people that believe the opposite. "Beethoven is great" is a widespread belief (nearly universal, perhaps), but somewhere there is a group that actively promotes the opposite. The fact that there is great variety in culture does not mean there is no culture at all. The phenomenon of culture is a result of *how* NTs learn, not *what* they learn or believe.

Cultural identity groups are possibly smaller and more fragmented now than in earlier times, but culturally derived identity is still the norm for NTs.

It may be helpful to define some related terms:

• Culture is the collection of symbols that a group of people share, including but not limited to words.

• The dominant culture is the one that is dominant in an area or nation.

• A subculture is a variation on a dominant culture.

• A counterculture is a subculture that defines itself in terms of the dominant culture as opposed in some way - as in the rebellion pattern.

Counterculture is not the same as being independent in the autistic way. Autistic independence means that a person lacks the exchange of cultural symbols (to varying degrees), whereas small countercultural rebellions of NTs are still using the NT patterns of friends & enemies, competition for rank and group identity, and so on, just like the NTs belonging to the dominant culture.

The plan

If a group of friends is going to do something, they have a plan, but "the plan" is a form of liquid truth, not a fixed plan. Someone in a social group might say "let's go see a movie" and that becomes "the plan" depending on their rank and confidence. If someone of higher rank says "I wanted to go out to eat," then that becomes another plan in the shared belief web - perhaps having a higher truth value, and pulling away the truth of the first plan. There may be other opinions stated, but the game being played is *not* one in which all opinions are equally valued, and there is usually not a vote.

It is important in an NT social group for everyone to want the same thing. The lower ranking members must spend their energy trying to figure out what the plan is and changing their stated opinion to the one that appears to be the winning plan. That way, they are sure to end up on the winning side.

NTs may refer to the plan simply as "it," or passively in some way. For example "that's how **it** is done," or "Marla is with us now; that's how **it** is," or "dinner will be at seven."

Sometimes, the last word defines the plan. If people disagree, the one who spoke last can be presumed to be the winner.

The phenomenon of "the plan" happens in families, friends, business, and just about any group. It occasionally happens that NTs will put social control onto the other person, or be overtly democratic. Consider these examples:

- "It's taco night. Let's go!" - This is the language of "the plan," spoken by a high ranking person, who has the confidence to create the plan, knowing that others will conform to it.

- "I like tacos, but I'll get whatever you want." - This would be spoken by someone who might be trying to buy rank, or who doesn't have the confidence to set the plan. A couple who is dating but who don't know each other very well may try to avoid setting a plan.

- "I'm going to get tacos. Who else wants some?" - This would be the wording of someone who is denying the system of rank (perhaps an autistic), or is in a situation where practical needs override social relations. For example, consider a sports team stopping on a long trip; being hungry and tired, they may omit the usual social considerations.

Religion

Religions are identity groups at one level. Although the truth in religions runs deeper than the current cultural norms, the choice of a religion has a lot to do with choosing an identity group to conform to. A clear example of this is the different branches of the Protestant religion, who all follow the same holy book and the same prophet. One of the reasons there are different branches is that there are different cultures, resulting in different behavioral expectations of the churchgoers.

Gender

Gender is often confused with sex, due to the lumping pattern (page 49). Sex is a trait of the body (female or male usually, but some intersex conditions also occur). Gender is a classification of language. (The word "he" is a pronoun in the masculine gender. In Spanish, "casa" is a noun of the feminine gender.) As culture is an extension of language, gender classifications of people exist in the symbolic web.

Gender is possibly the strongest single component of identity among NTs. When a baby is born, the first question asked is often "what is it?" The question is about the identity of the baby, which is assumed based on its sex. The phrase "Be a man!" does *not* mean to please have male sex organs; it means to conform to all the masculine things *associated* with manhood in the culture.

Women have gained rights and opportunities and in many respects are considered "equal" to men, but the groups have not merged into one. There is (in America) a strong assumption of what a person will be interested in and knowledgeable of, based on his or her gender, which extends far beyond natural differences of the sexes. A simple example showing the strength of these assumptions is that the toy sections of stores are divided into boys' toys and girls' toys, even for very young children. A great many details of NT behavior are determined by gender - for example, where money is kept (what kind of wallet or purse), how they protect their eyes from the sun, and the kind of soap they use.

Intergender communication is highly regulated in the American culture, to the point that there are three separate styles of language: between females, between males, and "mixed company" (a term that refers specifically to mixed gender, not any other kind of identity mixing). All-male or all-female groups might signal each other to change the style and topics when a person of the other gender comes in the room.

NTs actively regulate information about the body to limit it to the gender it goes with. NTs can feel offense at seeing the other body type or knowing some trivial fact that is related to the other body type (such as: a male NT knowing that Mary went out to get a new box of tampons.) The offense can be felt by people who are not even present: for example if school children were changing clothes without being segregated by sex, someone in the school office might be so offended just thinking about it that they would rush to the scene to put an end to it, in the very same way they would rush to prevent the children from hurting each other.

Unfortunately I have not been able to entirely resolve why the gender identity pattern is so strong in a way that fits in with the overall theory in this book. In the example of children seeing each other's bodies, the offended teacher probably believes that the children *are actually hurting* each other. By crossing the line dividing the identity groups, they are being *inappropriate* (refer to the common sense pattern on page 110), and therefore losing their identity. Referring back to the sexual tease pattern, it is essential to keep certain body parts covered in order to create competition, more potential mates, and ultimately, higher rank. If the females of the herd don't learn this pattern early, their rank will suffer in the long term. This social logic possibly extends to all information concerning the body and from there extends to information, interests, and attitudes of the two gender groups. Certainly a large amount of repression around sex is common, and this repression fuels huge areas of culture. Perhaps this vast repressed part of the belief web is what drives gender-specific objects like sunglasses and toys for toddlers.

Maturity

The NT patterns presented in this book are all learned, so there are people at all different levels of mastery. The most mature NTs have the most control over their display of feelings, the most confidence, higher rank, greater reputation, and more achievements. Crossing lines of maturity in relationships is considered inappropriate - relationships are supposed to be between people at the same maturity level, unless it is one of the relationship scripts that exists for the purpose of crossing levels (such as parent, teacher, mentor).

Like gender, maturity is a way to divide people into different identity groups and segregate them.

Brands and retail

Brands of consumer products are intentionally created symbols, and as such, have associations and beliefs that are tied with identity groups. Each brand and retail store has a target "demographic," which is a set of age, gender, and ethnic labels for the people they are wanting to sell to. NTs often shop according to their identity group.

Let's look at product categories in the area of cars. There are relatively fixed car types: sedan, wagon, van, hatchback, and so on. When the minivan was created, it created a new category, which was considered a risk: normally to sell cars (or anything) it is safer to stick with an existing category. Recall from the pattern of perception limited to existing beliefs (page 37), that a thing has to "be something," which is to say it has to be a member of category denoted by a cultural symbol. One of the car symbols is the sedan. NTs often can't tell you what a sedan is, even if they claim to know what it is. They know what they feel about it and what they associate with it, even if they can't define it. Toyota had at one time

178

a sedan and a wagon, both called Corolla, and another sedan and wagon, both called Camry. Instead of calling the sedan one thing and the wagon something else, they created the symbol "Corolla" to go with the middle class demographic and gave them a choice of shapes (sedan or wagon); and created the other symbol "Camry" for wealthier people, with its choice of shapes. All of this about cars is just to illustrate the pattern that brands are cultural symbols, and the market is defined by those symbols, not by what the products actually do.

Advertising is targeted to NTs, since they are the majority of earthlings. NTs tend to be susceptible to advertising because it mimics the type of cultural learning patterns that are explained in this book. The viewer of an ad may have trouble with independent thoughts, and may be distanced from evidence gained from her own life experience, and be only willing to learn new things in lockstep with others who are learning the same thing. Advertising plays right into these patterns.

The organization of supermarkets offers another way to understand how products are symbolically associated. The aisles contain groupings of things that are meant to be used together, or are culturally connected. Cans of tomato sauce that are meant for pasta are next to the pasta, but other cans of tomato sauce (or whole tomatoes) may be in a completely different part of the store. Religious candles are not next to birthday candles; even though they are physically the same thing, they are culturally different things.

Credentials

Credentials are rewards for achievement, and also serve as identity groups. A person can say "I am a PhD," which means it's part of the identity. Credentials give rank.

Music

NTs listen to music using symbolic filtering. Simple pop music is symbolic in the sense that its words, instrumentation, and other effects correspond to a genre, and the genre is associated with an identity group. The groups include such genres as R&B, metalcore, and Indie. Adolescents sometimes identify themselves as the genre ("I'm a ___"), particularly if it is a countercultural rebellion. Listening to the symbols in the music strengthens the associations with the listener's identity.

Fashion and clothing

The NT pattern of intentional display helps explain their preoccupation with appearances; they are not content to let their true appearance show; instead they must create it intentionally. Clothing styles and make up are used to display the person's identity group, and their compliance with *appropriate* dress.

The high-ranking cultural leaders compete with each other to define fashions, and the relative success or failure of their advertising constantly shifts what is defined as "appropriate."

Items of clothing are often specific to certain occupations and situations; people wear them because of who they are, and what they want to show, not because of the temperature or the need for protection.

A white swim top has to have enough difference in style from a white bra (even if they are made of the same materials, and have the same shape and function), so that people can tell which of the two items it is. A thing that looks like a bra in 2010 (and is therefore inappropriate to show in public) could be declared by a fashion designer in the following year to be a swim top, and then it becomes appropriate to show. This illustrates how clothing is used purely for cultural associations and not for function.

Not just clothing, but anything with a defined "look" is subject to changing fashions - for example, appliances, cars, purses, floor tile, and typographic fonts. The "design" of a car is considered to include only what the outer covering looks like, while the engineering includes what it is inside and how it works.

Changes in fashions are driven by economic competition more than by artistic inspiration. Designers have to constantly change, not necessarily improve, the looks of products. The difference in appearance between one product and its competitors only has to be great enough to allow consumers to distinguish it from the others.

Politics

Politics refers *not* to policy-making or governing, but to the conflict between ideologically-defined groups, and their relative power. All the activity around running for office and serving as an elected official revolves around building alliances, vying for rank within groups (political parties and related groups), and using the power you gain to serve yourself. "Friends" in the political sense are people that you give favors to and expect favors from in return. The purpose of having "friends" is to increase power and rank. "Gifts" in the political sense are purchases of friends. For example, a high ranking federal official might be friends with a high ranking state official. The federal official might influence budgets to get more money for that state, which is considered a political gift. The state official may then return the gift by supporting the federal official in the next election. These two people may have only met a few times but will publicly declare that they are "friends." Even though they are competing against each other for rank in the same party, they are helping each other because they believe it will help them both attain higher rank than the many other people in the party.

Do politicians ever fight for what's best for the people, simply out of a feeling of altruistic service? This may happen sometimes in a pure form, but more often in a less pure form with a similar effect. In an effort to win, politicians will adopt whichever opinion that they think will get the most support. In some cases humanitarian or altruistic policies are the most likely ones to gain support.

Hate crimes

We discussed trampling a flag a symbolic gesture. In the extreme, activities of this nature can be hate crimes, even if the activity is made of parts that are not individually illegal. For example, having a camp fire is not a crime, and dressing up with a cone on your head is not a crime, but a bunch of people with cones on their heads chanting around a burning cross *is* a crime because it is intended to be a threatening message. (In this case, it is a threat by the KKK to murder black people.)

Similarly, an actual crime can be considered worse if it is believed that the intent to harm was larger than the individual victim, and was a threatening message to a larger group.

Since there is no known way to measure intent, NTs assume that the behavior implies the intent. Refer to the pattern on Intentional display (page 98) for more examples.

Economy

While politics is the distribution or accumulation of power by law and by force, economics is the distribution or accumulation of power by money.

NTs often use possessions as symbols of their identity. The rich generally spend a lot of money on objects whose main function is to demonstrate their wealth. They may have two swimming pools even though a person can only swim in one pool at a time. The second pool is not primarily for swimming in - it exists to say "who I am." The fashions of the rich tend to become more complex, and their rituals more elaborate over time, in order to ensure that they cannot easily be copied by the less wealthy.

One organizing principle of the economy is that it arranges people by rank from poor to rich. The economy is built on the foundation of greed, which is not the need to have more *in total*, but the need to have more *than others*. People with the most wealth control the economy, and they are apparently content with the fact that some of their fellow NTs are living in poverty: the disparity is their reward for winning the economic game.

The great majority of NTs appear to be most comfortable placing themselves under the authority of a small number of leaders. They have a drive to conform their belief web to that of others, with the majority wanting to be in the majority identity group; consequently the whole herd tends to coalesce under the authority of a small number of symbolic leaders. Those leaders become wealthy from exploiting political loyalty and brand loyalty of products, and their wealth helps them maintain hegemony (group dominance) by mapping out the belief web that others conform to.

A common delusion is that the economy *exists*, as in "we need to fix the economy." That's a forest-first approach that can overlook the individual trees entirely. The trees in this analogy are the ability of each individual to meet their needs. The forest is "the economy."

The lumping pattern is evident when NTs assume that an indicator, like the Gross Domestic Product, is some actual thing (like houses), and value the indicator itself.

Identity laws

Identity laws are those that assume a certain belief web, and require interpreting free-floating symbols to enforce the law. Here are a couple examples of this vast topic.

• Many zoning laws allow and prohibit buildings based on their name, with the lumping assumption that their name is the same as their use and their effect on others. This relies on symbolic perception to enforce the law. For example, a zone might allow restaurants but not bars, or it may allow day care centers but not pre-schools.

• Some prohibitions are against specific identity groups, particularly those viewed as lower class. "No skateboarding" signs don't specifically prohibit rolling for conveyance, because their intended effect is to remove people whose identity group is "skateboarders," and occasionally signs will target the group (no bikers, etc.) instead of targeting the behavior.

• People who are gay are not allowed in the US military. The law is specifically against a person's identity or inclination, even though there is scientifically no dividing line between being gay and being not-gay.

Sports

Being a fan of a certain sports team is an identity group membership for many NTs, and a very powerful one. NTs can experience actual strong emotions from depression to elation depending on whether their arbitrarily associated team wins or loses. Playing sports is often but not always done in order to win and establish rank.

Social venues

NTs socialize a lot in order to learn and perpetuate the culture, and this is done nearly everywhere.

Certain venues exist mainly for that purpose, and other things (often food) are a secondary reason. Examples are restaurants, clubs, dances, parties, parades, and ritualized observances (weddings, funerals, flag raisings). Since there is no competing need for something to get done and almost no new perceptual information to process, NTs focus all their energy at these times into symbolic processing. That is, they aren't seeing or feeling the world around them with attention to detail, but are instead putting all their mental power into synchronizing their cultural symbols. They are using the social communication patterns (such as small talk, intense communication, fast communication), adjusting their liquid truth levels and aligning their associations in their symbolic webs, performing all kinds of display (such as personality construction, judgments, common sense, projection), and doing all of the relationship and power patterns (friends, rank, competition, moving towards sex or affairs, and the sexual tease).

All of this can even be done while there is constant high sensory input such as loud music, flashing lights, and smoke. Thanks to desensitization, many NTs actually find several hours of symbolic manipulation under these conditions to be quite refreshing.

Children

In order to make sure children conform to the culture, NTs spend a great deal of energy naming some of the most basic symbols and going over them repeatedly - such as the alphabet, colors, and weather patterns. Colors and weather exists in nature, but it is the *cultural associations* of color and weather that NTs are preoccupied with, not the natural phenomena. NTs teach things that are "true" (that is, shared) such as the fact that April is the rainy month, in the typical preschool calendar curriculum. Where I live it rarely rains in April, but that fact of the natural world is not the relevant point.

Dissociation between cultural lessons and nature.

Due to symbolic filtering, a preschool teacher in my area could conceivably give a lesson during April about April being the rainy month, and not even notice that it is in fact usually dry. This style of interacting with children is much like small talk, in the sense that it uses whatever topic is handy as an excuse to exercise the form of the teacher-student relationship category. The symbols that are taught in this overt prescriptive way are a tiny minority of all cultural knowledge, and there doesn't seem to be any requirement that the knowledge be correct.

Children's lives in NT families tend to be significantly organized around ranking/achievement activities like education and sports.

NT children want to please their parents. (I resisted believing this about NTs for a very long time.) Children use the make-feel pattern to make their parents feel proud by achieving external rewards.

Since gender roles are an extremely important identity group for NTs, the children are forced into them despite any other inclinations. Observing Americans, I can generalize that boys are most often normalized to the male identity group between ages 2 and 4. In that time, any behavior or dress that associates too much with girls may be strongly shamed, and parents may try to masculinize the boy by preventing playing with girlish toys and providing boy toys like guns and trucks. Girls are freer during the latent stage (which is roughly elementary school years) and are normalized later, between ages 10 and 12, when their boyish behaviors are shamed and exterminated.

Education of children in America is based primarily on the deficit model, which focuses on what children don't know yet. Success in educational policy appears to be defined as 100% of students knowing the exact same curriculum, and learning it at the exact same rate in the exact same sequence. Any differences in a student's ability to learn or in their interests is considered a problem for a system that is built for conformity.

Pathology & Disability

Since NTs are all about conforming to common beliefs and values, and they make everything a competition, it is especially hard for them to accept neutral differences between people. Differences are commonly judged as better or worse than the norm, rather than just identified as different in a neutral way. Autistic people are assumed to be defective because we're different; the concept of a difference and a defect are lumped in their belief web and it can be hard for them to pull those concepts apart.

Here are three ways of treating differences between people:

1. **Conformity.** The difference is seen as a defect that is intentional, and is therefore deserved, and can be fixed. Examples: "He's an idiot; he should get a clue." "He's autistic; he should just be normal."

2. **Medical** (diagnosed or pathologized). The difference is seen as a defect that is unintentional (something is broken), and is therefore undeserved, and cannot be fixed by the person. Examples: "He has an intellectual impairment." "He is an individual living with autism. (and will stay that way)"

3. **Typology.** The difference is seen as neutral. Example: "He can't do ___ (something specific) ."

In the conformity model, the person has a defect that he should be able to fix and is usually his own fault (according to the pattern of thought), while in the medical model, the person has a problem that he can't help and either it is permanent or he needs professionals to fix it. The culture defines a threshold dividing the normal and medical categories. For example, looking at intelligence, there is the category of "normal" and the category of "impaired." People are seen as being in one or the other identity group, but not between. If your intelligence is very low, say

IQ<70 (setting aside for now whether IQ means anything), then you "have mental retardation" or you are "intellectually impaired" or "special," and the standard of intelligence that you are judged by is low. But if your IQ is 70 or more, then you don't qualify as special, and the standard you are judged by is the normal category. So, if your intelligence is lower than average, but not so low as to be in a different identity group (say, 80), then you might be called names like an idiot or a dumb-ass. But those same name-callers might think it is inappropriate to use those labels for people in the impaired identity group.

The example above ties in with desert: people are thought to deserve the judgments that come with the labels applied to them. A full NT-style explanation might be "I can call person A an idiot because he's not actually retarded; he's just being dumb, so it is his fault, and he deserves it. But person B is a 'special-needs' person and has an 'intellectual impairment' which is not his fault, so it would be highly offensive to call him an idiot."

There is also a sex-related dynamic. Males who become emotionally unstable are more likely to end up in prison and be viewed in the conformity model (perhaps because they are more likely to hurt other people), while females who become emotionally unstable are more likely to end up in mental institutions and be viewed in the medical model (perhaps because they are more likely to hurt themselves).

The phenomenon of *diagnosing* someone puts her in the medical model. The phenomenon of *undiagnosing* someone occurs when non-professionals decide to put someone back into the conformity model (in their eyes), in order to remove the protective shield against verbal attack that is offered by the medical model.

The "typology" model is the thinking used when differences are seen as neutral.

Over time, specific traits move from one model to another. Left/right handedness, for example, was at one time more in the conformity model, and has moved into the typology model. The invention of the "Asperger's Syndrome" diagnosis moved some autistics from the conformity model to the medical model and contributed to the "epidemic" of autism.

What's an autie to do?

This last chapter is meant to help you, the autistic (autie) reader, find your place among the earthlings. If the foregoing description of NTs sounds bleak, you may be wondering if there is any hope of fitting in or competing with them. The short answer is probably "no," but you can still find yourself and make a place among them, perhaps even relate to them, without actually being the same as them.

In this chapter, I will share my views of autism, explain why you are at a disadvantage, and share some advice.

What is autism anyway?

Psychologists define autism as a defect, and more specifically, a list of behaviors that are defective... no need to repeat that list here. There are many problems with the list-of-defects approach. It doesn't distinguish between neutral differences and those that are a problem. (If a person stims a lot, is that a problem? Who is it a problem for? There is no single answer.) It doesn't interrelate the observable differences in any structure - it's just a list. It includes core differences alongside side effects. And the diagnosis depends on the judgment of the doctor using socially constructed measures (like being "odd") rather than unambiguous scientific measures. Consequently the definition of autism in common use is socially constructed - a free-floating symbol defined by its cultural associations.

There are, however, **measurable brain and muscle differences** that are correlated with the socially constructed diagnosis of autism. I'm listing these just to prove that autism isn't purely behavioral fluff, but is really *something* about the brain, even if the common definitions haven't quite settled on what it is. You would have to go to original sources to verify and understand these. A quick list is: autistics have (on average) larger brains, more and smaller minicolumns (certain brain structures), lower functional connectivity among cortical regions, less firing of mirror neurons, less small motor control, less development of the frontal lobe in the second decade, more use of the mental imagery part of the brain to comprehend low-imagery information, preference for low level processing, more spread of excitation, and various performance excellence in detailed tasks.

I will now give **my own working definition of autism**, which begins with the root of it and explains the way it develops in terms of the roots:

1. The root difference is that the autistic person develops a type of brain that admits natural *unfiltered* stimuli and does not filter it (as much) using cultural meaning. The person does not become desensitized, and continues

to see and hear and touch the world in a more direct way than NT adults do, because the symbolic filtering doesn't protect the senses against the world.

2. As a result of the root difference, the person is considered overly *sensitive* in typical NT environments, and learns to manage it by shutting down or other techniques. The autistic's stims and "problem behaviors" could mainly be side effects of being overwhelmed.

3. The person doesn't develop *language* or develops a lower dependency on language, because their inputs are direct, language isn't needed as a tool of perception, and the feedback between language, gesture, and all other cultural symbols to their perception is not developed. This helps explain the basic communication problems.

4. With a lower use of language, the person develops cognitive *independence*, and does not follow the herd. This results in being "in their own world" or nonconforming. If the conformance is very low, the person will be less able to learn from others, and will acquire a smaller generalized base of experience and knowledge, making it less possible for them to live independently. However, the cognitive independence can lead them into special interests which they can learn a lot about.

5. The long term effects of being *outnumbered* by NTs include (a) the person has little or no opportunity to be with others on their own terms, and thus fails to mature in interpersonal skills or depth; and (b) the

person is judged and coerced constantly by NTs, which is perceived as bashing; thus self-esteem falters, leading to chronic stress, anxiety, and depression.

The summary of this model (taking the italic words in the 5 points) is that autism is *unfiltered perception leading to high sensitivity, low acculturation, and cognitive independence.* I see the other "symptoms" listed by psychologists as side effects of that basic difference.

Common understanding of autism glosses over the difference between acculturation and socialization, saying only that autistics have *social* deficits. It is more accurate to say that autistics have low acculturation (we assimilate and conform less). While we don't engage in the socializing pattern (as defined in this book) as much as NTs, we might have as much of a need for connection to others as anyone else does.

It is not the issue whether a cultural norm is truly "normal" or not, in relation to a trait indicative of autism. For example, direct eye contact is felt to be appropriate in US culture, but in some cultures, it is considered invasive or threatening. Lack of eye contact is one of the signs of possible autism in the US, and that merely means that the autistic person is not conforming to the culture of eye contact. Even if the autistic person's trait is "normal" by world-wide standards, they are still exhibiting low acculturation by failing to conform to the immediate culture.

One autie correspondent of mine says

> "I believe that almost all of the things that are 'wrong' with AS people are just a result of a

poor culture-to-person fit, and of the snowballing fall-out from cognitive dissonance generated by the huge gulf between the fairy-tales NTs believe are The Truth and the actual observable data."

What she calls fairy-tales is what I'm calling socially constructed reality. Her main point is that there is nothing "wrong" with us, but the differences can cause major secondary effects, which may be commonly seen as "the problem."

She goes on to give a wonderful account of the emotional side of autistics versus NTs, and I'm including all this because it made me think a lot - although I'm still skeptical. She says

"Diagnosis works on us to make us doubt our own competence and to overestimate the competence of people who tell us we're doing something 'wrong.' But NTs are not, contrary to what they believe about themselves, 'better' than us at things like social skills, reading other people's emotions, or empathy. Not to say we're good at it - what I mean is that they're no more or less likely than us to be inherently good or bad at these things than we are. They're just bad at them in different ways, and those ways are less noticeable in this culture at this time because they're normalized; this is their culture, after all, so it's optimized for their particular aptitudes and deficiencies (put a lone NT into a convention or conference full of Aspies, and just see how 'competent' they are then!). They're also less capable of noticing when they do make errors, which further skews their perception of their own relative competence.

"The 'emotional difficulties' of AS people seem to boil down to 4 things, and none of them are about us being inherently defective. (1) we feel things - sensory and emotional things - more strongly than NTs; (2) we're more sensitive to other people's emotions than NTs, and thus 'catch' their emotions faster and stronger; (3) we cycle through our emotions faster than NTs (NTs perseverate emotionally); (4) we're given really really really (can I stress that again? *really*) bad data about what we and everyone else are feeling, which throws off all subsequent calculations and makes it impossible for us to get the 'right' answer."

A note about the "spectrum"

Most things that can be measured in animals exhibit a bell curve, shown below. You can measure brain size, motor control, memory, and so on, and with most of those kinds of measures, most people will fall within a certain range (the norm), and a few will fall below the norm and a few will fall above the norm.

This is what "normal" means: falling withing the tall part of the bell curve on any given measure. Many people insist that "normal doesn't exist" or that it depends on your point of view. But when it comes to measurable data points, *normal does exist*.

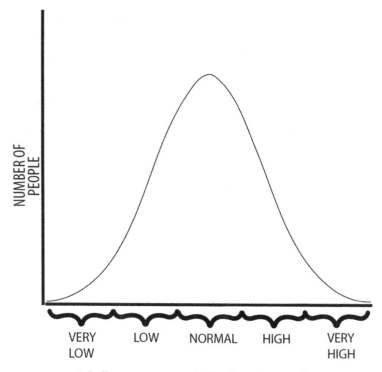

A bell curve represents the distribution of many measurable human characteristics.

Now if there is such a thing as "autisticness" which could be objectively measured (which there is not), there would be two sides to the curve, just like the curve above. It would be a "spectrum" from low to normal to high - a bell curve like any other measure. Most people would be neurotypical or normal (by definition), the right side would be increasingly autistic, and the left side would be increasingly anti-autistic, which I will also call associative. What would anti-autism be? It would be the extreme form of the traits that are opposites of autistic traits. For example, extreme dependence on language, associative thinking, a belief in socially constructed reality that overshadows the other kind of reality, and extreme herd-dependence.

If you have ever heard a political speech that seemed completely free of content, you are familiar with extremely associative people. Extreme associatives live in a socially constructed world and can use words for hours at a time, talk about words, twist words, and never "say anything" (from our point of view). They can talk about alliances, desert and other relational emotions, but might not say anything that counts as information to an autistic listener.

Going back to the spectrum mapped out as a bell curve, a measure of autisticness could potentially be a measure of the extent to which the brain admits natural stimuli. The normal range is where people balance language and nature; the low range is like the associative who only lives in language and can't see natural reality; the high range is like the autistic who only lives in nature and can't use words or see social reality.

A slight adjustment of the arbitrary line between the normal range and the autistic range can change the incidence rate drastically. It is as if you measure your house using a ruler with more closely spaced lines, and conclude that your house got larger. This phenomenon of measurement could explain most of the current "epidemic" of autism.

Since the 1990's, the world has learned that autism is not an on/off condition, and now understands it as a "spectrum" from low- to high-severity, or low- to high-functioning. The idea of severity could mean several things:

- More severe = appearing less typical?

- More severe = more impaired in daily life, or higher level of care needed? (But, "level of care" is not a trait of a person; it is an effect of the thing, not the thing itself.)

- More severe = fewer compensations developed?

The concept of the "spectrum" doesn't capture the variability in it. Some people need a lot more care than others simply because they have developed an interest in things that don't earn money, or because of physical problems that are unrelated to autism. Some have suggested it is more of a "landscape" with many variables, rather than a "spectrum."

Still, people want to know "how autistic are you?" (ignoring the complexity of the variables). Speaking for myself, I notice that some autistics are more socially developed than me, and some are less. Some are more sensitive, and some less. I don't really stand out in my own mind as being more or less autistic than others. We all take what we are and develop different compensations to interface with the world. It is the compensating strengths that others use to judge "how autistic are you," not the fundamental traits. I developed a lot of those compensating strengths that mask my condition from people meeting me for the first time, and I often feel like I'm living a lie by doing it. When I'm with someone who is judged as more "severe" - that is, someone who has not developed as many compensations - I usually feel like we are in the same tribe, even if I don't look that way to others. The bottom line is, don't trust what someone looks like as a measure of their autism.

Simplicity and authenticity

One area where auties have a natural advantage is in simplicity of our thought. Our thoughts appear to be less encumbered by emotions, and we intuitively know that language is an invention. We cannot lie as easily.

In the 1990s and 2000s, fixing autism has become a movement in health and education; hundreds of new books, teachers, and professionals of all kinds are coming to you to help make you different - to help you learn social skills, be less sensitive, and so on. If you are in this system, I feel very concerned and tender about you. I haven't given much advice in this book, and the main advice I want to give is to remain authentic - keep your natural advantage. Yes, please learn things, but please understand that the system of "help" is a manifestation of the ultimate pattern.

When you are being led into falseness or complexity, please resist. It is so easy to get lost there. Growth in the true spiritual sense cannot be measured by anyone else and is not the same as conforming. What you have to offer will *not* come from the shallow skills that you learn from the system; it will come from the depths that you already have. All the time you spend believing in the false notions of success and failure is lost time.

In *Black Beauty,* Anna Sewell says "If a thing is right, it can be done; if a thing is not right, it can be done without." This is my reminder of simplicity.

The meaning of meaning

NTs can have meaningful growth experiences together, of the sort that change the course of their lives. Here is a fictional example: Leading up to the senior prom in high school, a popular girl leaves her boyfriend, there is a big fight, social groups get rearranged, someone is expelled from school, and there is a party where people do things that are hilarious and relieve the built-up tension. If you went to high school, you can probably recall themes like this (or maybe you only heard of them indirectly) and hopefully you can recreate this type of group experience in your mind.

In those events, each person joins the fray in their own way - taking risks, winning or losing, and each comes out feeling like it was a pivotal experience that defines a stage in life and their place in it. "Things" changed, and it was considered deeply *meaningful.*

However, an autistic person who is witnessing all this may find there to be no meaning in it. What were the "things" that changed? What is all this "meaning" supposedly in those kinds of experiences?

The "things" are symbols, not actual things. The word "meaning" should be torn apart into three different levels: definition, intent, and relevance.

• *Meaning = Definition.* The definition is what symbols literally indicate or signify or point to (the signified).

• *Meaning = Intent or purpose of a speaker.* A baby's cry has a meaning even though the words are not symbols; the cry conveys the baby's intent. People can mean one thing and say another - that is, their intent is communicated while they say words whose definition is something else. Such as: "Get out" is defined as "exit," but in a particular situation, it could have the intent of almost anything, such as "that's surprising."

• *Meaning = Relevance*, usually with an emotional quality. It is expressed as the amount of meaning, not what the meaning is. For example, "Your apology meant a lot to me," or "Before my mother got cancer, the Clean Air Act didn't really mean anything."

While autistic people can deal with symbols, intent, and relevance, we don't necessarily experience mixing these together in a symbolic way as NTs normally do.

The following five points are ways that NTs are able to experience meaning. In the example of the high school experience above, all five of these could occur.

• Individual words are loaded with relevance by association.

• Conformance and adaptation change the self, and change is relevant to anyone.

• If meaning is inferred, it can feel deeper than if it is explicit. Inferences can defeat defense mechanisms, in cases where direct meaning would be rejected. Also, active learning is more relevant than passive learning, so the more work that goes into discerning the meaning, the more relevant it seems.

• If a symbol has more than one meaning, it feels deeper. For example, a father character in a book can be both a biological parent and a proxy for a heavenly Father.

- NTs may also reenact scripts that are known to be meaningful as a way to intentionally have a meaningful experience. Religious scripts, for example, are predictable ways to find meaning.

Why you will generally lose

For many autistics like myself, there is generally no hope in competing with NTs on their terms. We are not playing to win; they are. Even if we could give up our strengths and go to the basest level of NTs in some areas (for example, abandoning our love of accuracy and adopting a threat-based concept of friendship), that would still not enable us to adopt their strengths, such as sensory integration, and we probably would not be able to memorize their constantly-changing culture. So in that sense it is hopeless.

Take a work situation in which you (the autie) discover and correct a mistake, and in this case the mistake is a setting on a machine. You then deliver the message to a co-worker: "production will fail because the threshold was set incorrectly." Now, when an autistic speaker gives information like this without conforming to NT expectations of communications, it does not matter whether the information is correct or clear in a literal sense. The NT listener will hear the content related to *beliefs* and *influence* first, then the *informational* content later. The message given might be factually correct, but the message received might be equivalent to "It's your fault, you moron." If the recipient hears only threats to his identity, he cannot also hear the literal message. Thus you have started a conflict.

Autistic people can be mistaken as manipulative, uncaring, rude, even dangerous sociopaths. Once this impression is given, you are the enemy, and enemies who don't fight will lose.

Since you don't deal in culturally shared symbols, you can't manipulate the belief system of others. Since people are always competing for rank, they will manipulate the belief system of others, and the general consensus in a group may come to be that you are the cause of all the problems. If it is a setting where people are trying to be live up to high moral standards, you might just be the target of rumors; in groups with lower standards, the eviction or shunning could be more open and forceful. In either case, you lose.

Being labeled autistic can put you in the category of "not able to care for yourself," which is sometimes a technique of NTs to maintain power over you. The truth is: you can do *some* things, but not *everything*, for yourself. That's the truth for everyone because humans are social animals. It may become a collective belief that you can't do *anything* for yourself, which is never true, but if you can't manipulate collective beliefs, then you lose.

Why normal therapy might not work

There is a disconnect between the ideology of the mainstream helping professions and autism, which I will attempt to capture here. These are warnings. You may find someone who understands your condition well, and my point is not to disparage everyone in the field.

Generally autism therapy revolves around pretending there is no fundamental difference, and trying to steer autistics into acting NT. People see autism as the problem, and they see *acting* as the solution. It is not that they think only autistics should act; they believe in acting as a general path of development for everyone, and for a reason. NTs generally *decide* who they are in a social context, and so when they try to help you, they apply the same principles that work for them. But you are not a cultural animal. You are a sensitive animal. You will *discover* who you are, not decide. Huge difference! You must climb *your* mountain, not the one that a therapist thinks you should climb. The acting skills that you might learn to mask autism can be irrelevant or harmful to the process of self-discovery.

Schools may have an annual "diversity day" and claim to "celebrate" diversity but in reality, NTs feel sorry for people who don't conform, and they even feel it is wrong, and they label it a disorder that has to be destroyed. If you are in a therapeutic situation where your basic self has been labeled wrong, them you have been damned and that "therapeutic" relationship could hurt more than help.

Beware of casual advice like the following: *keep plugging away, expand the number of people you come in contact with, give it more time, relax, count your blessings, get involved with a club, develop a hobby, do things you are interested in, and learn social skills.* None of it is bad advice really, but none of it is the fundamental issue. Generalizations about self improvement that apply to NTs often do not apply to us.

You might be misinterpreted in a therapeutic setting. Recall the pattern on behavioral shortcuts - page 86. If you look down, your helper will assume you are sad, and if you do just about anything, your helper will assume something based on NT behavioral culture, which may be wrong. Therefore they might have a very hard time interpreting you, and will likely suggest things that are not relevant.

You might have been given misleading and confusing information about your emotions and other people's emotions. You might feel sad about something, realize you can't change it, feel frustrated, angry, or take whatever path you take in a short time. You might process quickly, but NTs tend to bind up their emotions with the symbolic web, and feel things with others in lockstep, bringing the processing speed way down. Your fast processing might be misinterpreted as anger about the original event, when it was really sadness or something else. If you grow up constantly getting wrong data about yourself, you may not have developed a good way to know what you are feeling.

You might be cut off from your verbal-intellectual side and be living in emotions and sensory experience, and be perceived as an autistic lost in her own world. Or, you may be cut off from your emotional side and be living in facts, and be completely baffled by every social situation. What is happening for you? The question in therapy is: What is actually happening? Don't get sidetracked by people telling you what they expect should be happening. If it sounds wrong, it probably is.

Many NTs like to protect you from the truth about yourself. If your extreme arrogance in 4th grade repels everyone, the teacher may hide this fact from you; she may try to keep you from learning that about yourself, and may ask others to pretend to be nice to you. If the other children are compliant, you can get confused and you don't learn from failure. For NTs, the truth can hurt (it threatens the belief web), so they might avoid it. But the straight truth could be better for you.

Understand in yourself the difference between a real strength and a compensating strength that masks a real weakness. You may have to climb down the wrong mountain in order to climb *your* mountain, and that could involve unraveling the layers of compensation. Compensations might include being highly verbal, being "right" about everything, being organized, becoming a public speaker or being funny. If you get points (grades, money, recognition) for your masking compensations, you may persist in incorrect beliefs about your true weaknesses.

Therapies commonly recommended for autistics include:

- *Copying the behavior of NTs.* If this is done well, it is called success by NTs who see behavior as equal to health. But it isn't true development.

- *Social stories.* This starts from a deficit model - that you haven't adequately learned the culture, and it must therefore be drilled in a slow remedial way. It is helpful to learn the culture of the people you live around, but it might be more effective for you to learn it from an anthropological point of view (like this book takes) rather than trying to trick yourself into internalizing it.

- *Rewards and punishments for good/bad behavior.* This topic deserves another book, so I won't even start on it.

A note on social rules: NT socializing is *not* built on rules, although some common autism interventions are based on that assumption. In their effort to get autistics to mimic this pattern, teachers might break it down like this: (1) First learn basic rules like saying thank you, asking to play a game, don't talk more than a few sentences at a time, and so on. (2) Later when the rules are learned, learn the exception to the rules based on context, such as: you don't have to ask to join a game during gym class, and it's OK to talk for more than a few sentences when you are giving a lecture. But this is *not* what NTs are doing and it is *not* how they learn. As stated in the socializing pattern, socializing is sharing, rehearsing, and synchronizing cultural symbols and associations. They are not following externally imposed rules; they are acting out the culture that they have internalized.

Autistic people do not see or internalize socially constructed beliefs (as much). The beliefs are far too numerous and dynamic to make explicit and teach one by one. Therefore, the effort to normalize autistics by teaching us culture by rote cannot work. One way to find out if a so-called rule is really a rule is to ask an NT to state the social rule unambiguously. You will often get answers like this:

- "Conversation doesn't always have purpose."
- "It's about just being polite."

- "It all depends on the situation."

- "You just have to learn to pick up on signals."

If they say anything like this, the "rule" isn't really a rule. They can't state the rule for the same reason they can't define "Victorian" - because it is a free-floating symbol that is defined only by its associations.

What therapy works?

It should be clear by now that I don't think you can or should be treated for autism. If you are depressed or stuck, get treated for what's bothering you, but *you can't get treatment to become someone else.* These are some mainstream or common alternative techniques that I feel have helped me:

- *Meeting other autistic people,* learning a lot about autism, and understanding the NT culture around me. Studying the differences gave me more confidence in my identity, and more self-esteem. I've learned to see the NTs as a bit weaker and more predictable, whereas before they were an unknown threat that seemed very powerful.

- *Saying "I love myself" out loud.* If this is hard for you to do, you can build up to it ("Meg loves herself" or "I tolerate myself"). It is is a good thing to be able to do, especially if it seems goofy. No one can give us what we are not willing to give ourselves, so start with basic love and respect.

- *Inner child work.* There are lots of books on this. I used my right hand (dominant hand) to write in my journal, then used my left hand to write from my inner child. The brain will actually think of different things to say depending on the hand that is writing. In my case, my inner child would often say general truths about love and be less stuck on my current set of problems.

• *Work on personality types.* In particular, the Enneagram has been very helpful. (I'm a Nine.)

• *Dream analysis.* I didn't get sidetracked into the questionable idea that each object in a dream represents something. What I learned that helped much more was that the objects are all swapped out by meaningless placeholders. The actions and descriptions mean something, but they are applied to the placeholders. The analysis work is finding the actual things in life that the dream's actions and descriptions apply to.

• *Acupuncture and tapping on acupuncture points.*

• *Compassionate communication.* See www.cnvc.org. This was huge for me because it unlocked some things about what we really need and don't need, which the wider culture is terribly confused about.

• *Exercise.* Irish and modern dancing for me.

• *Completing commitments that I made.* I found that if I had a lot of work and was under stress, that just doing it is the best way to lower stress.

Loneliness

Autistic loneliness appears to be very different than the kind described in most self-help books, if it is even included at all. The autistic kind of loneliness is derived from actually being isolated, while the NT kind is more of a temporary mental condition or delusion, and NT advice on this matter does not seem to get to the true depths of this problem as experienced by autistics.

The isolated ball is not interacting, in the billiard ball theory of social interaction.

There is a common theory of interaction that I call the billiard ball theory. People are like millions of billiard balls on a huge table. There is an endless supply of people and they are constantly coming into contact with each other and bouncing around. The common assumption is that just by being on the table, you will get hit by other balls - you will have some kind of contact, find a boyfriend or girlfriend, get useful contacts, and so on. The true part of this theory is that there are millions of people and you don't need any one of them; you can always move on and bump into other people. The part that can be false for autistics is the inevitability of crossing paths and making contact with those millions of other balls.

There are a few interrelated reasons why you might not be striking any other billiard ball on the table of life:

• First, you may be repelling them because you have scary mannerisms, or smell bad, or are very arrogant, or something else that sends people away before they get near.

• Second, you may be unwilling to make a symbolic connection. In my experience, most NTs will only make a relationship that fits into the part of the symbolic web that we don't have access to. That is, they require a relationship to be fixed in their web and have language and cultural associations - usually bound up with group identity and vying for rank. But you may be too independent. You may not be willing to make strategic alliances (what some NTs call friends). You may not be willing to manipulate people into being with you. If you won't do these things, you are not going to win attention from people who are limited to these types of relationships, and relationships with them are impossible.

• Third, you may have climbed so far up the wrong mountain, that there is no you in there. You may have become such a ghostly shell of a person that there is no longer a hard surface to clink against. Any relationship, no matter how transient, has to be between two connectable surfaces. If you are not connectable, there will be no relationships. If you lost your you from too much therapy that was aimed to destroy the autism, then you need to regain the autistic you.

If you are lonely and the best advice you get is "learn social skills," or "that happens to everyone" or something else that feels trite, you must trust yourself on the matter. If you feel that no one wants to be your friend, that is probably true. You must face reality and deal with the three things listed above. Most importantly, expose YOU and not a fake construction of what you think an acceptable person would look like.

If you are trying to fit into a group, beware of trying to relate to the group itself, as if groups had consciousness. The only relationship you can have is with a person; groups are side effects. Although NTs define their identity by groups, those NT groups are held together only by individual one-on-one relationships.

There seems to be a big difference between autistic people with a female body and those with a male body. The body you have attracts attention (or not), and can therefore affect your sense of loneliness. Autistics with a sexually attractive body may get too much attention (but perhaps only sexual attention) and may still be starved for genuine connections, or be confused about the difference. Those without that asset may suffer a lot from both lack of emotional connection and lack of sexual attention/connection.

Special interests

Some people will say your special interests are a problem, but I see them as the basis of your education. For example, if you memorize the names and numbers of the Apollo missions, people might think you have a "perseveration" on a boring and narrow topic, which is clearly of no use for a career. But should you avoid the topic? I think if that's all you do with the Apollo missions, you haven't really gone far enough. Maybe you should get *more* detailed with it. If you continue to learn the volumes of all the storage tanks and the family history of the astronauts, then the act of letting your interests take hold of you will give you expertise in certain detailed areas of knowledge. It will also reveal general knowledge of fields like history and physics through the particulars. If you go further still, and learn the pressure to volume ratios and whether they correlate with a fuel's carbon density, you begin to break through the extremely detailed into the extremely general. You are likely to find out things that no one else knows. Since we learn details and compose wholes from details, these "recreations" (hobbies, perseverations) can be the education that school doesn't provide.

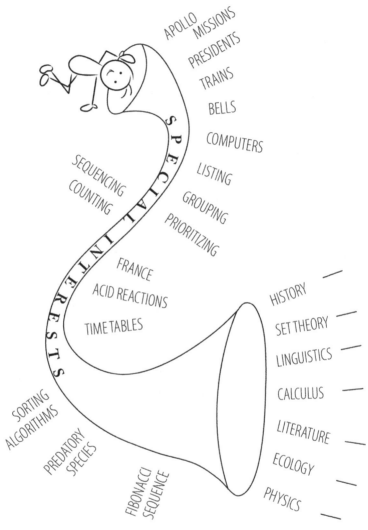

APOLLO MISSIONS
PRESIDENTS
TRAINS
BELLS
COMPUTERS
LISTING
GROUPING
PRIORITIZING
SEQUENCING
COUNTING
FRANCE
ACID REACTIONS
TIME TABLES
SORTING ALGORITHMS
PREDATORY SPECIES
FIBONACCI SEQUENCE

SPECIAL INTERESTS

HISTORY
SET THEORY
LINGUISTICS
CALCULUS
LITERATURE
ECOLOGY
PHYSICS

*The tunnel of special interests,
showing how a person breaks through
from the extremely detailed into the extremely general,
by going deeper into narrow interests.*

Final advice

Our time on this planet is limited, and it is filled with suffering. People may attack you; sometimes that is the best they can do from where they are. Most of them come from families who survived some kind of trauma - perhaps rape, drug abuse, or war, and we must forgive them. The repercussions of evil persist through many generations. It may feel impossible or dangerous to live from the heart.

You were not put here to act like everyone else or to be docile. You are independent and sensitive. The keys are within yourself, not in a religion, a treatment program, or a drug. Listen to your own calling in your own language, and follow. Follow the first littlest thing, one that does not overwhelm you or lead you to the lions. Following your calling teaches you to hear your own language. Get your confidence by being more autistic, not less; don't run from yourself in an effort to become typical.

Know yourself, and enjoy your stay!

On the Web

Enjoyed the book? Discuss and
read updates here:

www.afieldguidetoearthlings.com

About the Author

I live with my wife and two children in
Albuquerque, New Mexico. I'm self-identified
autistic person (or Asperger's), and I co-
facilitate a local GRASP support group (see
www.grasp.org). I work as a software developer
for my own company (see www.ianford.com).
Other interests include Irish dancing, growing
fruit trees, and transport planning. I write
about various interests on a blog here:
ianology.wordpress.com.

Made in United States
North Haven, CT
06 December 2022

28012618R00124